For all the unfortunate victims of sexual abuse, especially the children—Ally, June, Elly, and others like them.

PROLOGUE

This book is based on real and true events as remembered by me, Ellen Hahn. All the characters' names have been changed except for mine. It is my sincere hope that victims of sexual abuse, regardless of their ages, will forge through their pain and heartache to embark on a journey of hope and recovery through prayer, forgiveness, family, friends, and counseling. No child ever deserves to be sexually abused by anyone, and it's important for you all to know that true happiness is possible and attainable through the Lord's love for you. There is nothing inherently different about my daughter or me that makes our healing possible and yours not. Simply put, we are now truly happy, and you can be, too. Happiness and peace await you.

Live as children of light, "for the fruit of the light consists in all goodness, righteousness, and truth." (Ephesians 5:8)

Contents

CHAPTER 1 FOOTPRINTS ON MY HEART 9

CHAPTER 2 THE TRUTH SHATTERS ALL 19

CHAPTER 3 THE SILENCE BEGINS AGAIN 29

CHAPTER 4 THE THUNDER OF BROKEN SILENCE 37

CHAPTER 5 THE FAMILY SPLITS 42

CHAPTER 6 THE CLUES 52

CHAPTER 7 THE TIP OF THE ICEBERG 67

CHAPTER 8 THE COUNSELORS 73

CHAPTER 9 ALLY'S CHRYSALIS 85

CHAPTER 10 A NEW MAN! 90

CHAPTER 11 JUDGMENT DAY 97

CHAPTER 12 THE FALLOUT 110

CHAPTER 13 LESSONS LEARNED 117

CHAPTER 14 THE AFTERMATH 131

EPILOGUE 137

CHAPTER 1
FOOTPRINTS ON MY HEART

And if anyone causes one of these little ones who believe in me to sin, it would be better for him to be thrown into the sea with a large millstone tied around his neck. (Mark 9:42)

"My, my, Grandma,
What big teeth you have!"
"All the better eat you with,
 My dear!

   Yep, I was set up. No doubt about it. Set up like a con makes its mark. I was stealthily stalked and preyed upon like a tiger's kill, but, in my case, I was the naïve and young prey. Like other pedophiles the Abuser probably watched me and groomed me for sexual abuse. Of course, I trusted the Abuser, because he paid attention to me and spent lots of time with me. I was a youngster when the sexual abuse began. Here's how it all went.
   I was one of three children, the middle child, with one older brother, Peter, and a younger sister, Gwen. We lived in a rural neighborhood in upstate New York in a hundred-year-

old farmhouse that Mom was always fixing up. She put in new linoleum floors in the kitchen, painted the walls in the living room, painted snowy landscapes with a paint by number set, and planted pansies and Sweet Williams in her front flower garden. Mom didn't worry about us children coming or going, because the neighborhood seemed so safe, and typically, my older brother, Peter, and I just played close to home. But as time went on, we began to explore the surrounding neighborhood on our own.

The Abuser had soft brown eyes, dark hair, and tanned, almost leather-like skin, even though he was in his twenties. He was slim but barrel-chested, with sinewy arms covered with black hair. The Abuser was funny and fun to be around, and all the neighborhood kids, including me, looked up to him. He could do tricks like making a coin disappear and reappear. He'd gently toss an imaginary coin high in the air and then snap a large paper grocery bag to make us kids think the coin landed there. Like the other children, I would look into the bag wondering where the coin was. Then amidst wide-eyed looks, giggles, and the utmost wonder of us kids, he'd magically reach in the bag and pull out the coin! He drew realistic pictures of Popeye the Sailor Man cartoons on his bicep, which he would flex, making it appear like Popeye was moving. He also sported a large military tattoo on his upper arm. Yes, all us kids loved the Abuser and felt special when he took his time to notice any of us.

It, the first sexual episode, occurred when I was just three years old. I innocently took the Abuser's hand as he lead me to a musty-smelling room and lay me down on the towel-covered counter of the green and white wooden washstand. I fixated on the little chips of green and faded cream-colored paint peeling off the rustic washstand I was lying on, and with my fingers, I gingerly picked at the paint until I got a little chip loosened that I could flick off. Then I determinedly focused on my favorite toy, a little yellow-and-brown teddy bear named

Timmy. I clutched her close to my chest, hummed, and talked to her in a soft whisper voice.

"Timmy, later we will go out side. We will play in the dirt. We'll make mountains and tunnels and mud cakes, too. You and I will nap together."

The Abuser's voice was odd and guttural as he moaned. He spoke to me. "Elly, I need to feel you—it will make me feel happy. This is a special time for just you and me. You like spending time with me, right? I won't hurt you—you'll see."

Next the Abuser yanked down my elastic-waisted, red corduroy pants and my white cotton panties in one swift deft move and started groping my crotch with his hands! I was stunned and afraid all at the same time.

Next the Abuser deeply groaned with almost raspy sounds as he continued to finger me with one hand and rub himself with the other. The sensation between my legs was strange.

I spoke to myself, "Do I need to pee?"

The Abuser's touch was urgent and rough. I was afraid of the bizarre yet intense look in his eyes and his deep, throaty groans, but it was obvious to me, even at this young age, that somehow I was giving him pleasure. So I was happy, wasn't I? Still clutching my beloved teddy bear, Timmy, I knew enough to be quiet until his groans subsided. Mesmerized by the cracks on the ceiling, I remained detached. I hummed silently to myself and flicked paint until it was all over. I could hear the birds happily singing in loud and even shrill chirps. The soft breeze rustled through the heavily leafed birch and maple trees outside the small, dirty window. Finally finished, the Abuser warned me not to tell anyone about our special times, or they would have to stop.

Another special time I detached myself from the sexual episode by staring at a crack in the ceiling. How did the crack get there? How long was it? Then I pretended I could make myself so tiny that I could escape into the crack where no one would find me. I could go deeper and deeper into the crack and discover its inner self. Then it was over — until next time.

One special time led to another and another and another until the occasional special time became frequent occurrences. And before long, the sexual episodes increased in frequency, urgency, and intensity. The weathered old barn was just a quarter mile from my house. I remember special times in the milk house, the little rickety, rough-hewn eight-foot-square wooden room, attached to a decaying old dairy barn in our neighborhood. The mildewy old boards and sweet smell of freshly cut hay assaulted my nostrils, and the little cracks of light peeking through the milk-house boards mesmerized me during the special time, but then, the motley barnyard dogs all barked loudly harkening someone's appearance.

"Quick! Shhh!," the Abuser said. Then he hastily yanked up my panties, and the special time was postponed until next time.

Other special times were punctuated by the Abuser's scents and touches. I could smell his sweat. I could feel the roughness of his sandpapery stubble on my face and neck as his rough calloused fingers go tippy toe between my thighs and higher. Sometimes he made me touch him. Other times he rubbed his thing between my legs but never inside me. His breath was laden with the stale odor of beer and whatever he had for lunch. Sometimes I smelled hamburger and fries, other times fried onions and peppers. Usually now the Abuser would unzip his jeans and drop his deep-blue or green printed boxer shorts as he prepped me to rub him.

Like a wolf in sheep's clothing, the Abuser cunningly convinced me that we were of the same flock. We were partners. Buddies. Peas in a pod. He told me so. The Abuser told me repeatedly how much I liked what he did to me.

"This feels good, doesn't it, Elly? I don't let anyone else touch me here. We're our own team, you and me, sweet Elly. I don't hurt you, and you make me feel so good. You tell me if I hurt you, okay, Elly? I'll stop if you want me to. But you want these special times with me, don't you? You are a good little helper. You like to help me, don't you?"

I knew, though, that this was a question that the Abuser really didn't want me to answer. Even though I liked the Abuser I was afraid to tell him to stop. He might really hurt me or he might tell. So I just took the Abuser's hand and walked with him. He smiled contentedly and tried to make me laugh like the heady days before the sex started. We used to play games, tell jokes, and he would tickle me silly. But now I didn't feel like laughing or pretending to have fun with the Abuser.

This continued for about four years, until I was nearly eight years old. I was confused and upset. The sexual abuse didn't feel right, and the Abuser told me I could tell him to stop. My heart was in my throat as I uttered a little girl prayer for courage. "Please, dear God, help me. Please make it stop; I don't want to do this anymore." I practiced the prayer, but secretly hoped that there would be no next time. But, of course, there was. I summoned all the strength I could muster and blurted out in a quick loud voice, to the Abuser.

"I don't want to do this anymore; please stop."

WOW! I did it. I really did it. God must have heard my prayers! Yippee! The special times then miraculously and suddenly ended forever! "Thank you, dear God, for answering my prayer!" I jubilantly cried.

The sexual abuse ended as quickly as a wispy breeze sweeps over spring daffodils. What a silly fool I'd been! The Abuser was true to his word. All I had to do was ask, and it stopped! I was convinced that the sexual encounters with the Abuser were indeed my fault, because I hadn't the courage to tell him to stop earlier. I must be the BAD one. My ultimate punishment for being a bad girl was the ensuing profound loneliness. The Abuser simply just sashayed right out of my life.

The Abuser, though, left indelible footprints on my heart, representing a hollow shadow of his once-awesome presence. In the Abuser's wake, he left scars, open wounds, and a dull everlasting pain in my little-girl soul. My inherent trust and love was suddenly replaced by a brick wall that grew stronger from one day to the next. I had lost my dearest gown-up friend, my best friend. Our special times and other times were really over. I felt trapped. The Abuser affected who I was, and worst of all, how I felt about myself. Now instead of being trusting, outgoing, and happy I was scared, introverted, quiet, and miserable. I had a permanent ache of loneliness and anxiety in the pit in my stomach.

I wasn't prepared for aftermath of the abuse, for I felt abandoned, betrayed, and hurt. I became withdrawn, shy, frightened, and stressed. I would hunch over, cross my legs, rock back and forth, until the tension in my chest and head subsided. My mom called this rocking "hunching," and she caught me doing it. At eight years old, I didn't realize "hunching" was naughty. I was quickly and harshly reprimanded. My Mom looked at me as if I was a freak.

She was shocked as she said, "What are you doing, Elly? You stop that right now. That is a naughty thing to do."

I felt horribly dirty, humiliated, and ashamed. I continued to hunch, anyway, but in the privacy of the bathroom in our white, rundown, farmhouse, as I trembled with the fear of being caught. Finally, a few months later, I got up the nerve to tell my mom about the sexual abuse. She looked at me horror struck and dumbfounded. When words came, she looked at me with her brilliant green eyes sad and glazed over, as if she didn't even see me.

"You must be mistaken. You must be lying. Never talk about this again. You don't know what you are talking about," said my mom in a steady, even, and authoritative parent voice.

But I knew she believed me. I knew—because Mom

insisted that I go with her whenever she left the house or the neighborhood. Mom took it on herself to protect me the best way she could, the only way she knew how. She watched Gwen and me like a hawk in search of prey. She also insisted on knowing where Gwen and I were going every single time we opened the front door. This was quite a departure from the earlier days before the abuse, when we allowed to go wherever we wanted and to roam freely on the dirt roads, in fields, and in empty falling down barns, wooden sheds, and other abandoned dwellings in our rural neighborhood.

Both little Gwen and I were required to go with my mother to home parties, where my mom sold household cleaning supplies and products. It wasn't so bad, though. Gwen and I got to see the inside of other people's houses, and we always had homemade cookies or cake prepared by one of the women. Sometimes there were other children to play with, but Gwen and I were always within my mom's earshot and within the line of vision of her watchful green eyes. When we girls were old enough to ride bikes, my mom cautioned us not to ride up to the main road or to linger anywhere. Yes, Mom kept close tabs on us girls. My brother, Peter, however could still roam the neighborhood, because he was older and was a boy.

In desperation, I distanced myself from others and retreated into a world rich with books, school, friends, religion, and make-believe with my brother and sister. For a while, I drifted apart from others like a ship set for unchartered waters. I would read for hours. I liked the *Grimm's Fairy Tales*, but my favorite series was the *Nancy Drew* mysteries. Vicariously I could be Nancy—creative, bold, smart and, most importantly, well liked. I got lots of attention by memorizing all the names of the books of the Old Testament and the New Testament of the Bible. The memorizing gig worked so well I decided to memorize long Bible verses and Lincoln's "Gettysburg Address," and I would dutifully recite them on command.

I coped with the devastating sense of loss in several ways. Suddenly as I tried to bond with other safe adults, my grandparents took on a new importance. My grandmother taught me, through example, to believe in God. She invited me to stay with her every summer for a week of vacation Bible school. Her warm hugs and loving glances somewhat filled the void left behind by sexual abuse. Since I did not attend church regularly, I constructed a wooden cross surrounded by stones on a knoll in the cow pasture. Each Sunday, my younger sister, Gwen, and I would slip away together and pray by this cross. This faith instilled the love of God in my heart and through the bad times, I could still feel God's presence. I knew I wasn't alone.

Still, as a young child, I wondered, "Why did God allow sexual abuse to happen to me, and why did I experience special times that weren't really special at all?"

In third grade, I met Maria, and we remained best friends forever, both during and after the short years of childhood. Maria, who was also sexually abused as a child herself, shared her secret with me, and our friendship bond solidified as we held on to our sad secrets. We had sleepovers at each other's houses, went to summer county and state fairs, and fell in love with the Beatles, President Kennedy and beautiful Jacqueline.

In school, I became a model student and a people pleaser. I worked hard to garner positive comments from my teachers, and I was a diligent student and loved school. As a young girl, I decided to become a teacher because my teachers treated me so nicely, and my report cards always contained something about me being a hard worker. I received perfect-attendance awards, citizenship awards, and a few academic awards. Once I considered telling my teachers about the abuse, but I was afraid they would think I was a terrible little girl, so I just stuffed the memories of abuse deeper into my soul suitcase.

I formed a close bond with my rambunctious endearing

older brother, my sweet, active little sister, and my precious and loving grandparents. I took on the role of "protector" with my younger sister and the role of "playmate" with my creative older brother. My brother would create complex story plots for our teddy bears, which would have adventures in outer space and new undiscovered territories. Peter and I played for hours in our front yard and built little villages, lakes, and volcanoes. Gwen, with her bouncy, strawberry-blond curls and large pinkish glasses, would run with her sturdy legs through the spacious front yard. We would fall together in the grass, giggling, as we rolled over and over. We created blissful perfect homes, tea parties, and happiness for our beloved dolls. I also showered love on our dogs, a gentle German shepherd named Duke, a slobbering blue tick hound dog named Queenie, and a black-and-white rascally spaniel with floppy ears named Prince, who would shake snakes vigorously until they died.

I blamed myself for the sexual abuse, because I did not know where else to place the blame or what to do with it all. Surely, it must be my fault. I was a bad, bad, wicked little girl. If anyone found out about this nasty little secret, everyone would surely scorn me. I just really wanted to be loved. That shouldn't be so hard, should it? After all, the Abuser loved me, at least for a while, didn't he? If I memorized enough, and did well in school, adults would surely think I was something, and just maybe that something would turn into love. In short I was desperately trying to replace the love I thought I had with the Abuser. I was never able to capture the love I so dearly sought. Could I even recognize real love? Better not to even take a chance.

My life continued with the festering ugly secret securely locked inside of me for many, many, years, as I became the Great Pretender. I imagined my life wonderful and, in my mind, pretended to have a picture-perfect life. The relationship with the Abuser was over, but now the effects, the tentacles of abuse, had a firm grip on me. The Abuser had deliberately and selfishly spun an intricate web of distrust and deceit with invisible yet unbreakable threads woven into an inextricable fortress, which entrapped me for decades. In an effort to regain the early, sweet, halcyon, happy days before the abuse, I continued the pretense of being happy and constructed a perfect little world in my mind. Yet, in reality, I was wretchedly unhappy, miserable, and unbearably lonely. The sexual abuse, which lasted for fewer than five years, would, in fact, haunt me for many of my adult years and affect my relationships with others. A sacred trust was breached, which resulted in profound and devastating life experiences. I had no way of knowing the horrible fate lying in store for me.

Unbeknownst to me, I was a member of an exclusive club—a club whose members increase in numbers from generation to generation, and who go on to lead sad, dysfunctional lives that spawn unhealthy relationships. I was destined to marry a *pedophile*.

Prayer for Chapter One

Dear Heavenly Father,

I come to you today with a prayer of healing for all the victims of sexual abuse. Help us, God, regardless of our ages now, to have the courage to heal by allowing Your love to comfort and strengthen us every day. Help us to let go of our pain, give up our sadness to you, and live for today and tomorrow—not the painful days of yesterday.

Amen

CHAPTER 2
THE TRUTH SHATTERS ALL

Therefore each of you must put off falsehood and speak truthfully to his neighbor, for we are members of one body. (Ephesians 4: 25)

Humpty Dumpty sat on a wall
Humpty Dumpty had a great fall.
All the King's horses and
All the King's men
Couldn't put Humpty
Dumpty together again.

Here I was, thirty-some years older but not much wiser. I was, however, savvy enough to detect some trouble in the cool September afternoon, because things just seemed weird—weird like snow on a sunny day or sun on a rainy day or a cold bitter wind on a clear, blue-sky day. The air was thick with a gloomy, almost eerie heaviness, which belied the brightness of the blue Seattle skies.

It was a crisp sunny autumn afternoon when I returned home after shopping for school supplies for the startup of school. My active, sweet daughters, Ally and June, with their dark-brown, long tresses bouncing and reflecting golden highlights, ran to greet me in the driveway. Ally would be starting second grade, and June would be in third grade. Humming to himself, my husband of more than twenty years, Joe, was happily painting the garage doors, a project he had started before I left three hours earlier.

Hmmm. I thought it strange that he hadn't completed the task since he really wanted to get the project done.

When I nonchalantly asked what he and the girls had done while I shopped, he answered without meeting my eyes.

" I, umm, took a break from painting and played with the girls for a while. Then I decided to read as I ate some ice cream and cookies."

He still didn't look at me as he answered — what was he hiding? Was he lying? Something was not quite right. I hated the chilling feeling that quickly consumed me.

The atmosphere was strange, like the quiet dead stillness before a raging storm. Despite the sunny day, my husband's strange serenity and my older daughters' ensuing comments let me know that a storm was, in fact, brewing.

June approached me with her blue eyes gleaming as she grumpily stated, " Daddy made me play outside while he and Ally were in the house. When I went in, he and Ally were in your and Daddy's big bedroom with the door locked. He told me to go back outside and play. I wanted to play with Ally and Daddy, but *he* wouldn't let me. Humph!"

I froze and stiffened. My thoughts raced! Oh, no! What had been going on? Could this be my own history repeating itself with my husband having "special times" with our daughter just like the Abuser had with me? Decades had passed, but the dryness in my throat and the throbbing heart were startlingly in the present. No — I was sure that Joe would never sexually abuse our daughters. After all, Joe knew about my childhood abuse, and he frequently called pedophiles "scum of the earth" that deserved to be shot. Surely he wouldn't sexually abuse OUR sweet little Ally—would he? NO, NO, I was overreacting. Still, why would Joe and Ally be in our bedroom with the door locked?

Determined to put the matter to rest and prove my innermost suspicions wrong, I scooped up my younger daughter, Ally, and went into the downstairs den.

We settled on the couch, and I asked Ally, "What were you and Daddy doing in Mommy and Daddy's bedroom when I was shopping? It's okay, sweetie. Mommy needs to know."

I held her warm, still pudgy, little hands in mine. Ally's eyes were wide as she studied me.

She finally whispered, "Oh, nothing, Mom."

Whew! I am relieved! I hastily turned to leave the room, secure with the knowledge that my suspicions were not confirmed, when my daughter dropped the bomb.

Ally slowly murmured, "Daddy and I were just playing the tickle game."

Ally crawled on to my lap and buried her head into my bosom.

Terrified but determined to discover what the "tickle game" was, I asked in an amazingly calm voice. "Tell me about this tickle game, honey. Where does Daddy tickle you?"

I purposefully tried to remain calm with both my voice and my body language, so as not to alarm Ally. My heart pounded thunderously as I breathlessly awaited the answer.

Ally's dark-brown little head tilted down as she averted her big brown eyes.

"He tickles me on my tummy and my feet, but he likes to tickle me best here," she replied. She pointed to her crotch. She looked up and delivered another shocking blow. "He lets me tickle him too, down there. He lets me touch it. It's our special tickle time. I'm special; Daddy says so."

Horror struck, nauseous, and feeling a sudden weight hit

my chest, back, and head, I instantly vowed to believe her and confront Joe. In my eyes the still-sunny afternoon suddenly became dark, ominous, and cold. In a trance, we rocked back and forth, back and forth, back and forth, for several minutes. I held sweet Ally tightly, continued to rock her comfortingly in my lap, and tried to hide the panicky feelings whirling in my head. I quickly prayed for strength and clarity of thought.

I replied, "Ally, you truly are a special girl, but not for the tickle game your father plays with you. You are special because of who you are and all the wonderful things about you."

Her seven-year old eyes peered up at me as I continued, "What Daddy did was wrong, and it will never happen again. Don't be afraid. I will talk to your father tonight after you go to bed. Thank you for telling me the truth. You are very brave, Ally...I love you so much."

Ally snuggled closer and looked up to me with fear in her eyes. She whispered, "Daddy won't get into trouble, will he? I'm sorry, Mommy. He told me not to tell, 'cuz he would get in trouble, and so would I."

I fought back tears as intense anger welled up inside of me. With excruciating pain in my heart and turmoil roiling in me, I uttered another prayer in my head. *Dear Lord, please give me strength, clarity of thought, and the right words.*

I had to remain calm on the outside, so I didn't scare my sensitive and intuitive little daughter. My prayer was answered as my words tumbled out confidently.

"Oh, Ally, you will not get into trouble. This is in no way your fault. Do you understand that?"

Ally nodded.

I continued, "If your Daddy or anyone else ever touches you there or in any way makes you feel uncomfortable, you must tell me. I am a grownup and will do what needs to be done. Do you understand?"

Reassured, Ally then gave me a quick hug and ran off to

play with June. Zombie-like, I struggled to act normally as I made dinner. Between scrubbing potatoes and getting a pot roast in the oven I was intensely, deep-down angry and experienced a sadness that penetrated me even more than losing my dad to lung cancer 20 years earlier. Knowing that my sweet little daughter was sexually abused by the man I thought I loved, chose to marry, and had been married to for over twenty years was much more heinous than the Abuser's sexual abuse of me as a young girl.

While eating, I numbly wondered how it all came to this. As I pushed the carrots and pot roast into a lumpy pile on my plate, I studied Ally. She appeared normal, and as usual, she complained about eating her carrots. Oblivious to my thoughts and quiet demeanor, Joe enjoyed the pot roast and was self-absorbed. He didn't even suspect that Ally had shared the shattering truth with me. June talked about the start of school and the new outfit she planned to wear. The chatter continued. Lost in my own thoughts, I only half heard the mealtime conversation, which sounded like distant echoes that occasionally penetrated my inner sadness. The meal seemed agonizingly long. I played with my food and couldn't eat much. Finally, dinner ended, and Joe, full, happy, and unsuspecting of the upcoming confrontation, helped me clean up. We kissed our daughters goodnight, and as usual went to the kitchen to finish any undone kitchen chores.

In a monotonic and shaky voice unfamiliar to me, I began, "Joe, I want you to stop messing with our daughter. Or is it daughters?" My voice sounded hollow yet steely, like that of a total stranger.

Joe, totally caught unaware, jerked his head and intensely glared at me. With total shock written all over his face he threw down the white glove. His first tactic was, of course, denial. Joe's eyes got squinty as he tried to break my stare. I could smell his fear in my nostrils, but he knew not the strength of his foe. My eyes remained steadfast as I glared angrily at him. I felt the courage and strength almost bursting from my being. His chest puffed up as he took his stance. He sized me up much like he was playing a game of poker. Finally he chose another strategy. He decided to feign surprise and affect innocence.

He indignantly replied, "I don't know what you mean. (dramatic pause as he coldly gazed at me) What on earth are you talking about? Just because you were abused you doesn't mean..."

"Stop right there, Joe!" I shouted. I jabbed his chest accusingly with my forefinger and continued. "This *isn't* about me. Don't you lie to me, you bastard! Why are you bringing up my abuse? This is about what *you* did to Ally today while I was gone. This is NOT about my abuse! It's about you, about us. I *will* leave and take the girls with me. Tonight! Yes, tonight! I will leave now. (I didn't know *where* I'd go, but I know I could find someplace.) Ally has no reason to make any of it up. Tell me the truth about your little "tickle game" with Ally. NOW!"

I paused then repeated " NOW!"" I felt brave on the inside, but my shaking voice revealed the anger and the deep fear swirling and contorting inside me.

Joe blanched as he eyed me carefully. He reminded me of a cornered, wild-eyed rat, like the ones in the 100-year-old farmhouse where I grew up in. He desperately sought a way to squirm out of this predicament. Finally he exhaled and looked at me beseechingly. I held my steely stare. He then tried yet another maneuver. He looked wounded and pouted. I maintained my don't-give-me-any-shit stare. Suddenly he shrank and deflated like a poked balloon.

"All right, I did touch her, but I've never hurt her. And I have never touched June. You must believe me," he answered.

He looked away. I could taste his fear and then his resignation.

He rambled on and on and on with a glazed, faraway look

in his eyes. Like a death-row inmate seeking atonement prior to execution, Joe confessed. He desperately wanted to be cleansed and forgiven. Like the opening of a floodgate, Joe continued revealing not one but several sexual encounters with our beautiful daughter. The endless stream of words was so painful and horrific to me I could no longer bear to listen. I transported myself elsewhere. As Joe rambled on, I detached myself and looked for a crack in the ceiling like the one I had found in the old farmhouse decades earlier when the Abuser abused me. I can't find a crack but began to examine the texture on the wall as I looked past the confessor. I can't bear to listen to the words. My husband continued on with the diatribe for more than an hour.

Finally finished, Joe sat in silence awaiting my response. Silence. Silence. Silence. My mind raced ahead with crazy sad thoughts. Now I was the deflated one. None of this could possibly be true. This was not real. Surely it must be a horrible nightmare. Floating above the line that separates fantasy from reality and insanity from sanity, I was catapulted back into the present. *This is my life and I have children to protect. I have to get a grip! I struggled to maintain clarity of thought, but think I did.*

I thought and thought and thought. Out of fear, panic, and the powerful desire to hold my crumbling family together, I finally made a horrible and chilling decision. I willed myself into thinking this was just a one-time slip up. I convinced myself that Joe did this only once to Ally, and that we could work together to make the marriage work now that the ugly secret was revealed.

Although I am sickened with shame and cowardice, I made two vows: one to protect my daughter and the other to keep this ugly truth a hidden secret. After all, thirty years earlier I had protected my little sister from the Abuser, so I felt totally competent, capable, and well trained to protect my daughter from my husband. I could do this.

Joe desperately looked at me. He begged me, "Say something, Elly. Anything, please, please!"

Agonizingly, I uttered between clenched teeth, "Joe we've been married more than twenty years. I'll not leave you, but you must get into counseling right away. If I ever—EVER— hear of any future abuse or even the hint of abuse, I *will* take the girls and leave you. Do you understand?"

Joe sobbed as he clung to me. An icy chill raced through me as his fingers gripped me like talons. I felt the imprints of his fingers on my back.

He tearfully agreed, "Yes, I need you, Elly. I don't deserve you. I'm a bastard, a real scumbag. Hit me if you want. Go ahead. Hit me. It'd make me feel better."

This was very odd since we'd never hit each other during our years together. Deep inside I truly wanted to kick him in the balls, punch him, or do some kind of permanent damage, but I could not hit him. I'd not give him the satisfaction. If I hit him, he'd feel better, and I definitely did not want him to— not at all.

So he continued, "I'm so glad to have this all off my chest. We can make it now. I know we can, Elly. I really am a good dad. I love the girls so much, and I really am a good father except for that. I won't ever do it again, I promise. I'll look in the yellow pages tomorrow and set up an appointment with a counselor right away. It'll be okay; you'll see, Elly; you'll see. Th—th—thank you."

He looked relieved—almost happy. He was grateful that, for now, I was not going to tell the world our nasty family secret. Out of fear I had let him cleverly manipulate me so that we could hold on to the carefully constructed façade of a good man and wife, who lived happily with two beautiful and spoiled daughters in a big house in the country. I felt drained and horrible. I was rigid with fear. I was afraid of having my family's life crumble into a million pieces like poor ole Humpty Dumpty with no one, not even the king's men, to pick them up and put them back together again.

I had to protect my daughter from my husband, preserve my family, and somehow keep it all a secret. Yeah, I could do this. I *must* do this. I just had to be strong. I knew I had to do this alone, because God certainly was not with me. Where was my precious God? How could He have allowed this to happen to my daughter? Wasn't it enough that my Abuser sexually abused me? My heart was heavy with hurt, betrayal, and sadness. I also felt the great onus of guilt, since I decided to keep our nasty family secret to myself.

How could I have not known? I should have known what Joe had been doing to my beautiful Ally. I was a good mother who was very close to both Ally and June. I loved my daughters with a deep-down intense love. I had so dearly wanted them to have a safe, carefree, happy childhood filled with happy cozy days of laughter and warmth. I should have known…should've stopped it. Somehow it must've been my fault. If this all came out everyone would think I was a bad mother. I must be a bad mother to not have known about this. I'd lulled myself into believing that we were a happy, wonderful family—just like the fake happy family I so carefully constructed as a young girl after my relationship with the Abuser ended. After all, somehow I had unknowingly let this all happen, so it was definitely up to me to put it all right again.

I could tell no one. It was the late 1990s and, I knew if even a hint of this ugly family secret were to get loose, my "happy" family would be torn apart forever. Now it was up to me to be the glue to hold the jagged and fragile pieces of my daughter's life, my life, and that of my family's together. My husband's guilt had strategically and effectively been transferred to me, and I, overcome with fear and full of turmoil, allowed the transfer to happen.

Riddled with guilt, I shakily thought of the words floating in my conscious.

I'd told my daughter only a few hours earlier, "I am a

grown-up and will do what needs to be done. Do you understand?"

These words haunted me for months as I preserved the ugly truths that infected, poisoned the innermost core, the heart of my family.

Prayer for Chapter Two

Dear Lord,

Today I come to you for courage and faith. Although I feel betrayed by you, please help sexually abused children tell the truth to a responsible and caring person. Give them bravery and strength through Your love to tell the sad and painful truth, so they can shed the burden and pain. Let them feel Your love, comfort and guidance. Help them NOW, dear Father, so they will not carry the secret, the burden, and the pain of sexual abuse into adulthood like I did. Thank you for taking the burden and pain. Thank you for giving Ally the courage to confide in me and for me to confront my husband. Help me to protect her so this will never happen again. Help me to find you.

Amen

CHAPTER 3
THE SILENCE BEGINS AGAIN

What made you think of doing such a thing? You have not lied
to men but to God.(Acts 5:4)

Hush little baby, Don't say a word,
Daddy's gonna buy you a mockingbird.
And if that mocking bird don't sing
Daddy's gonna buy you a diamond ring.

For about two years, I did *not* do what needed to be done.
I did not report the abuse, nor did I tell anyone about the
horrible secret embedded deep in my family's fabric. Instead
of following my conscience I kept my word to Joe and
maintained silence to the outside world. But the "silence"
created a thundering chaos within me and my family. Two
days after Joe's confession, in an attempt to assuage my own
guilt, I made a couple of futile attempts to make myself feel
like I'd done the right thing by reaching out to others. First,
just two days after Joe made the shocking confession that he
sexually abused Ally, I called a governmental family
counseling service.

Lying, I started, "Hello! I am concerned about the child of a good friend. She confided to me that her husband of over twenty years sexually molested her seven-year-old daughter. She wants to keep her marriage intact, and she is sure that the abuse took place only once." I continued, "She was afraid to call so I told her I would call for her. What she really wants to know is this. Can she get help for her daughter and husband without her husband being criminally prosecuted or breaking up her family?"

The concerned woman on the other end of the phone call spoke slowly but clearly, "Once the abuse is reported by either her husband, herself, or the daughter, it must be reported to Child Protective Services. Then CPS will conduct an interview, complete an investigation, and make a report. The justice system will eventually get involved. This family needs help."

I restated my most pressing question.

"Yes, but will the family be split up? This is what concerns (pause) my friend the most. My friend's husband is horrified and vows to stop the abuse forever. If he voluntarily gets counseling and the abuse does not reoccur, is it possible to keep the family together?"

The woman answered honestly, "I can't answer that. Each case is different, but you must convince your friend to seek help for her daughter, her husband, and...herself. I understand she is afraid, but she must be responsible and..."

I had enough of this! With each of her words I was overcome with pressing guilt and fell deeper into despair. I interrupted her, "Thank you for your help. Good-bye."

I heaved a big sigh as I returned the phone to its cradle. Ashamed of myself for lying and for not doing the right thing by reporting my daughter's abuse to CPS, I let fear control my life and my family's life for nearly two years. What did the woman mean? Why would *I* need help? I could understand why Ally and Joe would need help, but certainly not me. I had nothing to do with it. I was just married to Joe and was Ally's mother. What could she have meant? And besides, I was protecting Ally, so Ally was okay now, right? I stuffed these questions away in the recesses of my mind like all the other bad memories packed in my heavy baggage, as I let fear run my life and that of my family. Fear prevailed for nearly two years.

Next, I decided to confide to a co-worker and dear friend, Heidi. I entered Heidi's bright and organized classroom. I walked over to her desk ,and I lied and told her half-truths.

"Heidi, I need your help. I think Joe may have sexually abused my younger daughter, Ally."

(I never refer to Ally as "our" daughter anymore; she is "my" daughter. Without telling him and consciously unaware of what I was doing, I wrote Joe off in my mind as being worthy of his parental rights. The children were my responsibility—not his.) I continued the half-truth to Heidi.

"I have no proof, of course. It's just a feeling. What should I do?"

Heidi, who knew Joe from a few social gatherings, seemed shocked. She eyed me pensively as she gathered her thoughts.

"Elly, you must be sure, you can't accuse Joe based solely on a feeling. Keep your eyes and ears open wide."

Then Heidi perceived the sadness under my cheery façade of normalcy.

"Oh, Elly, you poor thing, even suspecting your husband of such a thing must be horrible." She leapt up from her chair and hugged me warmly as I sobbed softly into her shoulder.

Joe kept his word and sought counseling. To appease me, he entered counseling for men having sexual problems, but Joe was no dummy. He never revealed to his counselor that he had sexually abused his daughter. Knowing that any mental health counselor was obligated by law to report any sexual abuse, Joe instead focused on issues with his own past. He became even more self-absorbed and distant from the girls and me. He came to view himself as a good person who made mistakes solely because of the tremendous weight and pressures put on men in "today's society." According to my husband he was unhappy because he had to shoulder so much responsibility, including being a son, husband, and father.

Riddled with guilt, my past came back to haunt me. Not only was I to blame for my Abuser's sexual abuse of me as a child, I now felt like I was responsible for Joe's sexual abuse of our daughter. This thought caused chills to run down my back. Oh, no, what a mess!

Joe enjoyed the attention parsed out during counseling. He began taking anti-depressants and started helping more and more with household chores. He attempted to fill the role of a father rather than that of a playmate with our daughters.

When I questioned him about whether he was abusing Ally anymore, he bored holes right through me with his penetrating looks and spitting words, "No, you've got to trust me. It's stopped. It really has. Do you honestly think I'd continue doing that? Go ahead. Ask Ally."

I don't answer him, but the truth was that I didn't trust him. Not anymore.

I felt like throwing up as I asked my daughter, "Has Daddy played the tickle game with you anymore?"

I was so afraid of hearing the answer. Would she tell me the truth? Maybe Joe's bribed her with Polly Pocket toys, stuffed animals, and chocolate.

Ally looked at me and knew it pained me to ask. She touched me softly on my arm as I drove her to piano lessons.

Her words were direct, "No, Mommy. He hasn't. I'm brave now. You've helped me to be brave. I won't let him."

Even so, I continue to ask every few weeks. I hate asking, because I'm always afraid of what her answer will be. My guilt increased because I realized I didn't deserve the love and trust of Ally. What did she mean that I helped her "be brave"?

I tried hard to never leave Ally alone with him, but the realities of life prevented me from guarding her and protecting her from Joe 100% of the time. After-work commitments and other obligations filled me with anxiety and chills as paranoia and fear overtook me. Even though the girls were alone with Joe infrequently, I was terrified on the few occasions when he was "in charge" of the girls. When I went to the hospital for routine surgery that went bad and resulted in a 2-week hospital stay and a second surgery, I was deeply concerned about my daughters. Haunting questions tormented me as I hazily drifted in and out of consciousness. These scary questions rolled around in my brain like clothes tumbling around and around in a dryer that never shuts off.

I asked myself over and over again, "Oh, no! Will Joe behave himself when he is alone with the girls? Will they be safe? Will Joe try anything? Will Ally relent? Will Joe turn to June if Ally doesn't comply? Even if he doesn't do anything, will he be thinking it? Will Joe and I ever have sexual relations?"

I must get well. I must get well. I must take care of June and Ally.

Eventually, on a cold, December, frosty morning, I was on the road to recovery and Joe came to the hospital to take me home. On the way home Joe said he'd kept up with everything at the house except laundry. I came home to about 12 loads of laundry needing to be done! I wondered to myself how come he didn't have the laundry done. I worked full time and managed to parent, prepare meals, and get the laundry, yard work, and housework done. The whole time I was in the hospital he took leave from work so he had plenty of time to keep up with housework. Especially since church friends and neighbors provided meals for my family when I was in the hospital. He chose to have himself a mini-vacation while I was in the hospital! He sat at home, ate cookies and ice cream, and read books in between his obligatory short visits to me in the hospital. Once I was home, since I could not lift anything for several weeks, another longtime friend, Mari, came over and did all the laundry and vacuuming. I didn't deserve such great friends as Mari.

During the drive home I ruefully thought of the past few three months since Joe confessed to me about his abuse of Ally. Joe had dutifully taken about two weeks off from work to spend time with me in the hospital. But the reality was that he slept late, stopped in for a short visit in late morning, and brought June and Ally in to see me in the afternoon. Joe rarely said much to me during the hospital visits, and was busily reading paperbacks. My sister, Gwen, and my long time friend, Mari, were more attentive and caring than my own husband! My high point in the hospital was seeing the girls after school. Nine-year old June asked, "Mama, are you going to die?"

"No, dear, I'm not going to die. It will just take awhile for me to get better," I replied.

Relieved, June and Ally read me stories and jabbered on and on about their school day. They played with the hand-held electronic games I'd received as gifts from my sister, Gwen.

Several months later, based on a recommendation during counseling, Joe tried various anti-depressants until he found one that seemed to work for him. Unfortunately, though, after taking it for several weeks, he proclaimed himself healed. Subsequently, he took himself off the medication. He thought he was a failure when he was on the anti-depressant, because, as a man, he should be able to handle life's ups and downs without any medication. Like many chronically depressed people, Joe convinced himself that he didn't need any medication. He felt he was fine just the way he was, and others just had to accept him. He didn't have a problem — other people did.

Joe became more and more withdrawn from the family

and became a computer junkie who spent hours each evening on the computer. Eventually he came to bed, sometimes at 3:00 a.m., even on a workday. This was extremely unusual for Joe. In the more than 20 years I'd known Joe he always liked his sleep. What was the hold the computer had on him? I was suspicious, but just didn't care enough to pursue his reasons. At the time, it never occurred to me that he was hooked up with kiddy pornography on the Internet.

I tried to act lovingly toward Joe, but just couldn't. In the ensuing months I grew to despise him. Like a cancer, the hatred grew little by little until the very sight of him after a day's work made my skin crawl. We shared the same bed, but eventually, I couldn't cuddle with him or touch him. Worse yet, though, was the fact that Joe didn't even appear to notice my withdrawal from him. He just didn't seem to care. He was so self-absorbed that he hardly noticed my existence. I, riddled with guilt, felt anxious as the ever-growing despair hardened in my gut. We kept up a front for the girls. We'd give each other an obligatory kiss and ask each other questions like, "How was work today? Want to go to a movie? What shall we eat tonight?" Idle conversations. The girls were wrapped up in their own lives of school, art lessons, and music lessons. I, too, kept myself busy, busy, busy. Busy at work, busy with my daughter's lives, busy with church activities, busy with yard work, busy with decorating my house. Busy with anything and everything so I didn't have to deal with the underlying and omnipresent pain that punctuated everything I did.

I tried so hard to put the pieces of our lives back together to resemble some form of normalcy. I was sure Joe was no longer abusing Ally, but his former abuse had penetrated everything in our household, and its talons gripped me like a hawk clutching a rabbit. I was tormented, unhappy, fearful, and felt like a failure because I couldn't make our lives happy.

I prayed daily for forgiveness and guidance, but felt totally undeserving of God's love. My conscience told me I had not done the "right" thing in the eyes of God or society. I was miserable and ashamed. I was a *bad* person undeserving of anyone's love. I struggled with letting go of the fear that totally engulfed me. I knew we were a big ole mess underneath the façade of our fake family. I cradled Ally when I kissed her goodnight and guiltily felt the weight of the hushed truth.

No one in my fragmented family was happy. My husband's sexual abuse of my daughter was a formidable foe, one that I could not imagine away.

Prayer for Chapter Three

Dear Father God,

Today I ask all the grownups to receive Your courage and love so that they can be strong enough to report a child's abuse of any kind to the proper authorities. I especially ask you to give mothers the bravery needed to report their own husband's abuse of a beloved child. Help these mothers to report abuse immediately and not be afraid like I was. With a heavy heart I also beg for forgiveness for withholding my daughter's truth for too long.

Amen

CHAPTER 4
THE THUNDER OF
BROKEN SILENCE

Then I acknowledged my sin to you and did not cover up my
iniquity. (Psalms 32:5)

When the pie was opened
 The birds began to sing
Wasn't that a dainty dish
to set before the king?

 Things were wrong in the family, especially for Ally, whom
I observed carefully. She seemed despondent and strange.
Little by little Ally pulled away from the family and began
living in a pretend world of her own. She played with her
Polly Pockets, her baby Pinkie Doll, and read her books. She
played school with June, rode her bike, and continued to take
piano lessons. She threw her arms around me, clung to me,
and was abnormally quiet. She was introspective and said
very little. She just wanted to be close to me. I cuddled with
her and held her, but her sadness remained. She became

painfully shy and clung to me. It was apparent that she was a very sad little girl. Ally rarely laughed or beamed with joy. She had lost her silliness and oddball sense of humor. She was literally wilting before my very eyes. Acquaintances seemed genuinely surprised when Ally spoke, and mistook her silence as girlish shyness. But I knew, didn't I? *I knew why Ally was shy and quiet.* I knew, because I'd behaved the same way 30 years earlier. I knew the ugly, sad truth, and chose to hide it. By doing so, I got exactly what I deserved, misery and a wretchedly unhappy family.

Clearly, the time had come for me to step up, be heard and finally "do the right thing." Reality hit. My wonderful family was no longer wonderful at all! Truthfully, I had to admit to myself that my family hadn't been wonderful for a long time—no matter how hard I tried to maintain my desperate fantasy of a happy little family. This realization catapulted me into a frenzy of renewed vigor and courage. Clarity of thought prevailed. For the first time in months I felt alive and good. I could already feel a sense of joy and freedom, because I was determined to face the gripping fear and finally, finally do the RIGHT thing!

No longer would I put myself in the valiant guardian position to ensure that Joe would never be alone with Ally. Somehow I'd told myself it was all okay if I protected Ally from Joe, but what I'd actually been doing was making a justification for not dealing with the fear of the consequences of making the disclosure. I sadly realized that I could not guarantee that Joe would never abuse my sad, sweet Ally again. I was a fool for even thinking that I could fully protect Ally from her father. How stupid of me! I really knew that things could never be the same again.

As much as I tried, I knew I could not hold my fractured family together. Our family had become a textbook case of dysfunction. Joe was in a world of his own and spent hours on the computer, Ally was lost in her books and make believe,

June was active but sensed something was wrong in the family, and I let myself be controlled by guilt and fear. The damage had already been done nearly two years ago, and despite my great skill at pretending everything was wonderful, it was painfully clear that I had to let go of the fear that gripped me ever so tightly. I had to get help for Ally. Strangely, it was Ally's sadness that armed me with the arsenal of great courage that had eluded me for nearly two years. Finally, no longer able to deal with the crushing guilt of the ugly secret that festered underneath the threadbare fabric of my family, I prayed for courage and clarity, picked up the phone, and called CPS, Child Protective Services. With a pounding heart, burning chest, and a prayer for strength, I did it—I finally told the truth that had been locked inside of me and imprisoned my family.

"Hello, my name is Elly and my husband, Joe, sexually abused my daughter nearly two years ago. I have some questions."

The male voice on the other end of the line sounded young but helpful. I never did find out his name. He informed me that I was, in fact, doing the right thing. He commented that my voice was shaky and was patient with me as my questions tumbled out.

"Since the abuse was over two years ago and no further abuse has occurred since then, will my husband be criminally prosecuted? *Why do I care if he'll be prosecuted? I hate myself for trying to protect him.* And will our family be split up? What will happen to my daughter? Will case workers make her feel awful by having her rehash it all?"

He then told me that he didn't know whether my husband would be criminally prosecuted or not. It depended on the specifics of the abuse. He told me a CPS worker would come to my house and file a report. He didn't know whether my family would be split up or not because each case was different. My husband would probably have to go through some sort of treatment program and would have to stay away from children for the duration of the treatment program. My daughter would have to answer questions and go through some medical examinations. He also told me that according to Washington state law, the caseworker assigned to our case would have to notify the county police as a way to protect other children. The fact that the abuse happened so long ago and has not reoccurred would probably be a positive factor for Joe.

I then asked a final question. "Is it better for Joe to call and make the report himself?"

The CPS representative indicated that it would be better for Joe and for my daughter if Joe made the actual report.

"Okay, I'll have him call you back in about five minutes," I answered.

I called Joe away from his vegetable garden, and gave him a synopsis of my conversation with the CPS representative. Settled down on the brown, nubby, upholstered couch in the den, Joe looked at me with squinty, wary eyes as he hung his head like he wanted to squirm away, but I quickly dialed the number of CPS and handed the phone to him. He made the report as he waved his hand motioning me out of the room. Even though the door to the den was closed, I heard Joe lie and downplay the abuse. He told CPS that the abuse had been only a one-time occurrence. He stated that only a little bit of touching went on between himself and Ally. I hoped this was all true, but shivers went up and down my spine. Something in the way he spoke told me he was lying. Questions flooded my mind — How many times did Joe abuse Ally? How old was she when it all started? Did he ever abuse June or was he lying then? How much of our marriage had been a lie? How many other ways had he betrayed our daughters and me? The darkness of the past haunted me as vague memories of the night nearly two years ago when Joe rambled on and on and on about his sexual abuse with Ally. Nonetheless, I felt relieved.

With the choking bonds of secrecy broken I felt an unfamiliar fleeting wave of goodness and almost happiness sweep over me. I was moving closer to God, but kept a safe distance from Him just in case He should desert me. Now the whole mess was in the hands of the legal and justice system. I thought the really bad stuff was over, but I had no way of knowing how horrible the next two years would be.

Prayer for Chapter Four

Dear Heavenly Father,

Today I ask for your comfort and healing as the legal process begins. Ensure that Joe has consequences for his sexual abuse and that Ally feels relief and safe. Help me to accept your forgiveness for trying to protect Ally by myself and being afraid to report my husband's sexual abuse. I especially pray for the endurance of all the children and parents who go through this whole process. Help us all to shed the pain of being truthful to helping people in our legal system. I also thank you for the blessing of Your love and your constant encouragement. I rejoice, Father, because You gave me what I needed to tell the truth.

Thank you!

Amen

CHAPTER 5
THE FAMILY SPLITS

From now on there will be five in one family divided against each other, three against twoand two against three. (Luke 12:52)

Ring around the rosies,
A pocket full of posies,
Ashes, Ashes,
We all fall down!

I really didn't know how everything would unfold after the CPS report was made, but it totally changed our lives. We were caught up in a whirlwind of activity that ultimately ended up with my family being split as a flurry of counselors, police detectives, social workers, CPS caseworkers, attorneys, and health officials became commonplace in our daily lives. I quickly became a single parent and lived in the country home with the girls while Joe moved into a townhouse in a neighboring county. Not only did we live apart from each other, Joe and I began to build lives totally independent of each other. I grew stronger emotionally and was actually relieved not to have Joe in our daily lives. No longer did I have to wonder whether he was abusing Ally. I didn't need to put on the façade of happiness. Here's how the emotional split happened.

The day after the abuse was reported I made an appointment for my daughter, Ally, to begin counseling. Her sessions would start in two weeks. However, I was the one to get counseling first. Strangely enough, Joe and I had made three appointments for marriage counseling about a month before the abuse was reported to CPS. Our family doctor had recommended a good local psychologist who helped couples who had marital problems. So, as fate would have it, two days after CPS was notified, I sat in Mr. Bueler's office. (Joe refused to come because he was ashamed of his sexual abuse of Ally). Mr. Bueler was about 50 years old and had an office in his home. The office was full of warm colors, a cozy couch, and a clinician's desk and chair. He greeted me warmly and asked, "Why are you here today?"

Like a floodgate opening, my words gushed out. Finally, shed of the cloak of guilt and fear, I told Mr. Bueler everything. I told him that I could hardly stand being around Joe and how horrified I was about him abusing Ally. I also told him how I wanted to protect not only Ally, but Joe, too. Mr. Bueler explained that Joe had manipulated the entire family so he could satisfy his sexual needs. Joe's sexual desires with young girls had, in fact, become an obsession, an addiction. He told me that there was nothing wrong with me, that it was not my fault, and that my husband Joe wanted sex with young girls, not with adult women. He said that Joe might never desire sexual relations with a woman because Joe was a pedophile. I felt nauseous—it was the first time I'd ever heard someone tell me that my husband was a *pedophile*! Mr. Bueler stated that Joe had probably had problems with pedophilia for many years.

Then Mr. Bueler asked me if I wanted to remain married to Joe. I'd not really thought much about this, but I pensively answered, "No—I don't think I do. I was 20 years old when I married Joe, so I feel like I've always been married to him. I'm not sure I could let go. I feel sorry for him and feel like I'd be dumping him during this horrible time. I think he needs me more than ever now."

Mr. Bueler urged me to think about the divorce issue. Since we had two more scheduled appointments, we could discuss this further during the next session.

The second and third sessions with Mr. Bueler came and went, and with them my decision to divorce Joe was solidified. New fears overtook me. How would I provide for two young daughters? Where would we live? Would there be enough money? I had a full-time job, but Joe made nearly double the income I did. These fears were, however, little baby fears compared to the ugly fear I had dealt with for nearly two years ago. I was guided by the stark reality of what really needed to be done. Tearfully, I prayed soulfully for the first time in months. I felt I now deserved God's attention and love, because I finally lifted the guilt and burden from my soul by finally reporting the sexual abuse. I knew somehow things would work out. Armed with renewed courage and strength, I returned home from my last appointment with Mr. Bueler and informed Joe that I wanted a divorce.

I spoke clearly. "Joe, I want to talk to you privately. Let's go into the den." He eyed me carefully as he cautiously followed me into the den. My fear accompanied me. I smelled the fear and tasted it, but I was determined to broach the topic of divorce.

"What is it now?" he hastily stated.

I blurted out a reply. "I cannot stay married to you any longer. I can't trust you. We need to get on with our lives— apart from one another. I don't think you've truly loved me for a long time. And I don't mean just sexually." (We'd never had much sex in our marriage, and when we did Joe seemed totally detached.) Tears spilled down my cheeks as my body shook.

Joe looked at me and was silent for two excruciatingly long minutes. Shocked, he spat at me, "What about everything we've worked for? We have this beautiful country home on three acres, a motor home, and a wonderful lifestyle? Do you want to piss that all away?"

Then I was shocked. He said nothing about *us* only about "stuff." I sadly looked at him and said, "Joe, that's only stuff and things. I can't stand it! You're only interested in STUFF! I can give it all up and very easily too. I want peace of mind and happiness for all of us, including our daughters. I know it will be different for each of us financially. We've not been happy for a long time. Surely, you must admit that. But, please, look me in the eyes. Can you honestly tell me that you love me?"

He looked puzzled and genuinely sad. He slowly replied, "I cannot—I'm sorry. You're right."

I felt horrible. Every single day of our marriage he told me that he loved me. Every single day! He lied to me daily for years! My heart was thumping. "How long has it been since you've really loved me, Joe?" I asked.

"It's been a long time, Elly. I'm sorry," he replied.

My mind raced. Bitterness engulfed me because I'd expended so much energy and heartache in our relationship over the years.

I shot back, " How can you say that? I've stood by you for nearly two years and tried to make a go of it. Now you tell me you've not loved me for a long time, possibly years! It's true that since I found out about you and Ally I've grown out of love with you. Each day I love you less. I feel sorry for you. It's so hard for me to be in the same room with you, even now. We really need to get on with our lives. There's no love here any more. So let's cut each other loose."

Joe then slyly took another tack, knowing that he might be

able to get at me through my love for Ally and June. "What about our daughters? Divorce is never a good thing for kids. You know what the research says, Elly. It will have a detrimental effect on them forever! And what about finances? We've got a second mortgage on the house, a new truck to pay off, and really big charge card bills to pay. What about our plans for this property? We just got it cleared and are getting ready for horses. Do you want that dream of yours to come to an end? We'll both be poor! Oh, my God, Elly! Have you really thought about this?"

He still didn't get it. I looked at him with fire in my eyes and sadness in my heart. "This is not about stuff and finances. It is about you and me. We *do not* love each other. We are not happy. We do not live in a happy house. And as for our daughters, Ally and June will be better off without us being married, because I can't trust you, and there is no love between you and me. And as for finances and the rest, it'll work out somehow. It won't be easy, but I'd rather be poor than live in a loveless marriage."

Finally he gave in, shrugged his shoulders, and averted his eyes. "Well, we'll have to tell the girls and our parents," he said.

"Okay, let's tell the girls tonight and call the relatives tomorrow," I said matter of factly.

I was all jumbled up inside and terribly sad, even though I knew I was doing the right thing. If it was the right thing why did I feel so bad?

Telling Ally and June was much worse than I ever expected. June, with all the emotions a nine-year-old could muster up, ran from the living room horrified.

She screamed, "Why are you dong this to me? I've been so proud to have a mommy and a daddy that aren't getting a divorce like so many kids at school. Now I'll be one of *those* kids who have divorced parents! It's not fair!"

Ally just looked sad as we reassured both of them that our

divorce was in no way their fault. We told them how it wasn't entirely due to the abuse issues in the household. The reason was that no matter how much we tried we did not love each other and could not live together any more, because we were very unhappy.

June fired us a question, "Does that mean you'll leave me if you don't love me anymore or are *unhappy* with me?"

Ally looked down and quietly wept as she heard the news. We dealt with their shock and reassured both of them that they would be taken care of and that we would not leave them.

Weary and sad, I nonetheless felt the heavy, dark, cloak slide off my shoulders. The heinous secret of the sexual abuse was now in the open, and I was in the process of getting a divorce from an intelligent, kind, but manipulative and sexually messed-up man. I felt the pain of June and Ally press on my shoulders. The fear of the unknown future and the horrible realization of the mess my daughters and I were in created an omnipresent sharp pain in my stomach.

Despite all this, I had a calm inside me. I finally felt worthy of living the life God had given to me. I was on the path I was supposed to be on. Joe and the whole life with him was a detour gone dreadfully bad—very, very bad. Prayer, guidance, faith, friends, and the love for my daughters gave me the incredible strength needed to survive the next grueling months.

Little did I know that "doing the right thing" would be unbelievably painful and scary. The very thought of being a single mom with two daughters was an awesome and frightful reality. Would I be able to support them? Finding a new place to live, selling off everything to pay credit-card debts, a truck payment, and a second mortgage was overwhelming! Getting a divorce was indeed the "right thing" given my circumstances, but it was nonetheless a sad and draining experience. Dealing with divorce attorneys, police detectives, CPS counselors, physicians, and several counselors created a hectic pace. It was as if my daughters and I were stuck in an out-of-control revolving door!

The CPS office contacted me a few times on the phone and finally, a case worker came to meet with me about three weeks after Joe reported the abuse. The CPS representative was a pleasant-looking woman in her forties with dark, short hair and a frazzled, harried expression on her face. She greeted me warmly at the door and sat down at the kitchen table. From an over-sized bookbag, she pulled out a copy of the CPS report Joe had made on the telephone. She began by asking several questions about the abuse and took notes as we spoke.

She asked if Joe had moved out yet. Three days earlier, Joe had, upon Ally's request, moved out of our home into a two-bedroom townhouse about 25 miles away. I'd sold the truck, and Joe bought himself a used Mazda RX7 to console himself.

He told me, "Elly, I deserve this sports car, because I've had to give up so much, the house, the motor home, the truck. I need something just for me."

I was sickened by his attitude. How could he be so selfish? But, I sadly realized that his life and our marriage were built around his needs and the accumulation of material things. In contrast to Joe's sports car, I borrowed a friend's very old military green station wagon, which we lovingly called "Sherman" due to its resemblance to a military tank!

Joe's move into his own place was based upon an earlier telephone conversation with the CPS representative. She asked me if Ally felt comfortable with Joe living in the same house with us. I then asked Ally whether she wanted Joe to move out or stay with us. Ally surprised me by asking that Joe move out, and Joe further amazed me by moving out without a scene.

The CPS representative then asked whether Joe visited Ally and June. Joe and I agreed that he could visit the girls on weekends and some evenings. She spoke very seriously and said it was okay for Joe to visit the girls under one circumstance. Joe was to *always* be within my direct line of vision. If I was not vigilant, and Joe was left unsupervised with my daughters, she made it very clear that June and Ally could be taken away from me and placed in foster care. I felt confident that I could be vigilant in always keeping Joe within my line of vision. Keeping Joe and the girls always in my line of vision proved to be more difficult than I first imagined. Even though he came to visit the girls only three evenings a week and one weekend day, the constant vigilance wore me down. To make matters worse, Joe greatly resented my watchful eye. He angrily groused, "I don't see why you always have to watch me. I've not touched Ally sexually for over a year, I'd be foolish to do so now."

I painstakingly replied, "I will not jeopardize losing Ally or June by having them placed in a foster home. If you want to continue to see the girls at all, you have to abide by this rule. It's not my rule. It is a rule mandated by CPS. You cannot be alone with the girls under any circumstances. You lost that right. Do you understand?"

He answered me with a resentful, hateful look and shook his head in disgust.

For four months I kept a watchful eye on Joe while he visited the girls. But when Joe began seeing a community-based therapist and counselor, Lucy Moore, who worked solely with sexual offenders and their victims, his visits with June and Ally came to an abrupt end. Ally, June, Joe, and I were planning on taking the girls trick or treating on Halloween in the neighborhood where the girls and I lived in a smaller, but new home.

However, on Halloween day, I got a phone call from Lucy Moore. She was extremely concerned that Joe had continued seeing the girls and was adamant about Joe having absolutely no contact with either Ally or June. I was flabbergasted. Lucy told me she had spoken with Joe, and it was obvious that even though Joe had not actually touched Ally sexually, Ally was still very much of a sexual trigger for him. He constantly fantasized about her and was sexually aroused whenever he was with her. Just a few days earlier when Joe and the girls made jack-o-lanterns, Joe was getting sexual thrills by seeing Ally in a midriff shirt! Lucy said Joe fantasized about how flat and sexually appealing Ally's stomach was!

She was only nine years old! I was nauseated and amazed! I had unwittingly thought that since the abuse had stopped that it was over. How naïve of me to believe that, somehow, Joe could turn off his sexual problem and be normal. I was wrong, wrong, wrong!. What I learned over the next year and a half about pedophiles, sexual abuse, and its cycle opened my naïve eyes and ears. All contact between Joe and the girls ended. Joe was not allowed to ever see Ally or June again, unless they desired to see him when they became adults. Joe began treatment with Lucy, and I began to participate in her victim-support group.

Painful times and joyous times were abundant in the following hectic months. The most painful of all included questions posed to Ally by highly trained and empathetic policewomen, the extensive medical exam my young daughter had to undergo, and the horrible truths that Joe eventually confessed to. He had indeed abused Ally in many ways for several years! Weekly, during the support group counseling with Joe's counselor, Lucy Moore, I learned specific details of the many sexual encounters he had with Ally. I also eventually learned that Joe had, in fact, had a history of sexual problems long before I knew him!

Thankfully our lives were sprinkled with joyous times, too. The most joyous times were seeing the changes in my young daughter, Ally, as she broke out of her shell and emerged a chatty, smiling, vigorous little girl.

Prayer for Chapter Five

Dear Lord,

Today I ask for Your love to give me and my young daughters hope. As I face divorce I worry about how I will support my daughters alone. I know it is right to divorce Joe, but I didn't know all the turmoil would be so hard. Please give other wives the strength, courage, and patience needed to start new lives. Help abused children and their siblings cope as they make many changes in their childhood lives. Please God, help us all to hold it together.

AMEN

CHAPTER 6
THE CLUES

Jesus replied, I tell you the truth, everyone who sins is a slave to sin. (John 8:34)

Whatever happens twice
Is sure to happen thrice.

It's incredible how my love for Joe blinded me from seeing the amazingly clear signs of pedophilia. I didn't see them, because I didn't want to. Now, of course, I can look back on our 20 some years together and readily identify behaviors that were clear clues to Joe's pedophilia. As I look back with startling clarity, I wonder how I was so oblivious to the fact that Joe was attracted sexually to little girls. The simple truth is that I ignored what I saw because didn't *want* to believe there was anything wrong. So I bought into all his lame explanations and rationalizations. He was very clever and knew exactly how to manipulate everyone, including me. As a result, he successfully hid his secret for nearly 40 years!

Early on when we were first dating there were clues that should have stopped me from continuing a relationship with

Joe . We met while I was attending college in a small state teacher's college in upstate New York. Joe's sister, Angela, was one of my best friends, and she arranged a blind date for her brother and me. Joe turned out to be funny in a droll, dry, wisecracking way. He was intelligent, well mannered, opinionated, and arrogant. At first, I did not like him because of his arrogance, but gave him a second chance, because he was intriguing. We began dating regularly. Joe came from a large Polish-American family with lots of relatives who celebrated life with big holiday meals.

Whenever Joe greeted his younger sister, Angela, he remarked, "How's every *little* thing Gracie?" They would exchange a secret, tantalizing look. Angela slipped up once and said to me quietly, "Joe's hung like a bull, isn't he?"

I thought for a moment and then asked, "How do you know, Angela?"

Quick to recover, Angela replied, "You know how it is—living together as a family, I accidentally walked in on him once as he was getting out of the shower and couldn't help but notice. That's all."

I had encountered clue number one, and I should've followed my inner voice and quit the relationship right then and there. I knew something wasn't right in his relationship with his sister. I knew Joe had some secret in his past that haunted him. Later, after Joe and I were divorced, I learned that Joe, six years older than Angela, had molested Angela when she was still a young teenager. Although I did not find out about the abuse with Angela until after I left Joe, I should have gone with my gut instinct that "something was not right with Joe."

Joe and I did not have sex until we'd dated for six months, but during that time he kept telling me, "I'm going to get you, you just wait and see." I tried to hold on to my virginity (whatever was left of it after the Abuser's earlier abuse), but eventually gave in to Joe. He fumbled and acted like a virgin, but it was an act. I found out later (after Joe and I divorced) that he'd had sex before. He was nearly twenty-five years old when we first had sex; I was 19.

During our dating, we became intimate sexually as well as mentally. We were of different minds and backgrounds, and the contrasts between us were many. I studied for hours every day to maintain good grades, whereas; he graduated second in his large high school class and rarely needed to study to attain great grades. I went to a state college. He attended MIT and was studying to be an electrical engineer. I was the daughter of a telephone lineman. He was the son of an accountant. I was from a decent but not financially well-off family. His family had the appearance of wealth (3 children in college, beautiful clothes, a family vacation home in the Adirondacks on a lake, and a large two-family home in town.) Politically, he was a right-wing conservative and I a bleeding-heart liberal. I participated in freedom walks and marches— "Power to the People"—while he was part of *the Establishment*. We'd heatedly argue politics and the Vietnam War over a glass of wine and pasta. Then we'd happily make love.

Finally, things came to a standstill in our relationship. Out of the blue, he wanted to break up. He tried to tell me how we were getting too serious, and how he wasn't good enough for me. I was devastated! I'd given everything to this man, even sex! He was the only man I'd ever knowingly had a sexual relationship with. I was raised to believe I should have sex with a husband, and since I'd been intimate with Joe, of course, we would have to get married. I'd not allow him to dump me as casually as one tosses a dirty shirt in the laundry.

So, instead, we agreed to get married. Two days before the wedding I knew I should not marry this man, this Joe. My gut said, *NO, NO, NO!* It just didn't feel right, but I made a promise to get married. Surely I was just nervous. So I chalked the uneasiness up to pre-wedding jitters and went forward with the wedding. I was 20 and Joe was 26. **Clue number two was the overwhelming uneasiness prior to our wedding.** God was speaking to me, but, again, I chose not to listen.

Right off the bat, he was adamant about not having any children. In fact, he seemed to despise children. Although this bothered me, I forged ahead, telling myself that eventually he'd want children, but I vowed not to have children until he was ready.

Just two weeks into the marriage our sexual relationship *stopped*! A total screeching halt—kaput, done, over! I had no idea why. I'd just had a birthday and turned 21, and he was 26. We were both young, and I was an eager, willing sexual partner. **Clue number three was the abrupt end to our sexual relationship only two weeks after we were married.**

I tried many tactics to get our sex life back on track. I'd be frank with him and try to discuss it. I'd tell him how good it was and how we needed to keep our sexual life alive throughout our marriage. He'd get angry and storm off. I tried pretending I didn't care. I tried lavishing him with attention. I tried sexy negligees. Nothing worked. I later discovered that at 21, I was just simply not the young college girl he loved, but rather an adult "wife." As such, in his mind, I was no longer attractive to him sexually. At work or with his friends he'd pretend that we had a great sex life, and when other men made passes at me I'd lie and say I was happily married. In the deep recesses of my mind I felt again at fault. There must be something wrong with me or it must be something I said or did. It was my challenge and quest to figure out what was wrong with me, and then everything would be fine with me. Then my fake Cinderella happiness would return. I knew I must be unworthy and would have to live with a sexless marriage. **Clue number four was the fact that Joe chose not to have a sexual relationship with me**

during our marriage. We had sex only during the time we tried to conceive children (15 years into the marriage), and even then it was done clinically and matter of factly.

We both pursued careers and graduate degrees to keep ourselves busy. Joe still wanted no children and seemed to hate kids, even ten years into our marriage. Then as he approached his late 30s and early 40s Joe changed! He began noticing children. Whenever we had a party or a gathering Joe always gravitated towards children. The same children he had yelled at to keep off our lawn he was now inviting into our house to go in the hot tub or play air hockey and bumper pool! He started showing special interest in young neighborhood girls. He wrestled with girls on our front lawn and relentlessly teased them. He horsed around with neighborhood girls in the hot tub. Throughout all this, I rejoiced. He finally looked happy again, and he was not harming anyone. I thought Joe's change in attitude towards kids was simply a "mid-life change." Sometimes, though, something just didn't seem right. I thought maybe in his newfound happiness that there would be a revival in our sex life. But, we very rarely had sex, and he seemed to enjoy his time with the neighborhood girls just too much. **Clue number five was Joe's sudden attitude shift about children and the way he acted like a playmate with the neighborhood children rather than an adult.**

Then, I found some evidence! While cleaning closets, I found three pairs of girl's panties stuffed in an old brief case! They were NOT my panties and were not new.

When I confronted him about this, he reluctantly admitted, "They belong to one of the neighborhood girls. I took them from her drawer one time when you were house sitting for her parents."

I was shocked and horrified. Our neighborhood girls were only 11 years old! He regularly wrestled with the neighborhood kids and frequently invited them over to our house. We'd known our neighbors for over 10 years. I was astounded!

I stupidly asked, "Why would you stuff her panties in a briefcase? You're weird, sick! Ugh!" I felt like throwing up. Something was really awry here.

He got very angry and red-faced. He fired back, "What I do is none of *your* business! I like having these panties. They help me sexually. And I'm not hurting anyone. *You* are overreacting. It's not a big deal. I don't go out fucking around, and I'm a good husband and provider. I work hard."

What did that all mean? Confused and hurt, I somehow felt it was my fault for making *him* feel bad! I dropped the whole incident, but I replayed the incident frequently over the years in my mind. **Clue number six was the discovery of the neighbor girl's panties stuffed inside Joe's old briefcase.**

Then when our older daughter, June, was just a month old, I found a record album underneath the seat of the car. The picture on the album is that of a young, naked, prepubescent girl. It was artfully done with swirls of color intermixed across the glossy album cover. It actually reminded me of the colorful psychedelic depictions of the hippie era.

Again, I confronted him with this, and he was uncomfortable, but simply explained it away, "Oh, that helps me when I'm stuck in traffic. It gives me something nice to think about. Don't get wacky about it. At least I don't go out with other women or beat you. Don't make a big deal out of this."

Again, I felt nauseous. **Clue number seven was the picture of a naked prepubescent girl on the cover of a record album.** Apparently, he got some sexual satisfaction from the picture and perhaps used it while masturbating.

Then a few months later, I was paying the phone bill and noticed an hour-long conversation with someone in California. It was a call Joe had made from work and charged to our home phone. It was not a phone call made to any of our relatives who live in California. He said it was just a work call.

I pressed on. I knew if it was a work call that his employer would pay for it. Joe refused to tell me about this until I gathered all the evidence. He stuck to his story about it being a work telephone call.

He grumpily stated, "Sometimes we need to pay for the calls ourselves. The company will only pay a certain amount each month for phone calls, so lay off!"

I knew he was lying, so I replied, "Oh, come on, Joe. Do you really think I'm going to believe that? I know you don't have to pay for business-related phone calls. You never have. Why don't you tell me what this is all about?"

Joe walked out in disgust shaking his head and mumbling under his breath about how it was only *his* business. I called the number and found out nothing. But eventually a few weeks later Joe got some pictures of skimpily dressed young girls in an alluring pose in the mail.

I found out that he could receive mail-order soft porn. Joe simply called this number and through a series of questions he could order pornographic pictures of young prepubescent girls. He could order hair color, age, outfit, and a specific sexually alluring pose, and for a fee they would send him custom photos of young girls dressed according to his order in sexually seductive poses. Although he requested his mail-order photos be sent to a private post office box, by mistake the photos were sent to our home address. When confronted, Joe's shoulders slumped, and he confessed to the previous (California) phone call and his request.

He sounded very innocent. "I got the number from some guy I know, and the girls aren't naked. I thought it would help me sexually. *And*, besides, no one is getting hurt. Lots of guys do this. It's totally normal. Come on, you know I don't mess around with other women or anything. I'm a good husband. The girls are not *naked* or anything. *Geez!*"

Shocked, saddened, and amazed, I replied, "What's wrong with you? I'm attractive and love you. I've tried repeatedly to have a sex life with you. But you're never interested, and all you want to do is jerk off by yourself! I think it's sick that you have to have these pictures. These girls are children! *And* more importantly now, we have a baby daughter, June. I will not allow these things to be sent to the house. June could discover them! You need to clean it up, Joe."

Joe carefully constructed his response. Finally he gave me a steely look and said, "Elly, I will not have these things sent to me at home. I don't want June to find them. This has nothing to do with our love. I love you and June and would do nothing to hurt you or her. I don't see any harm in what I'm doing. It has nothing to do with you, and—besides—I'm going to do what *I* want."

Sadly I replied, "Sweet little babes is what it takes to sexually arouse you? We will never have a decent sex life. I can't compete with little girls that are 12 years old! This is not right. It is *not* normal. This is sick pornography!"

Joe then angrily replied, "You will never understand. You don't even try! Just shut up! This is not pornography. The girls are not naked! I *am* a good husband and a loving father. So what if we don't have a sex life? Lots of couples don't. We can still love each other and make a great family. Don't spoil it all by overreacting to a few harmless photographs." **Clue number eight was the whole incident of the pictures of the young girls and Joe's denial that he was using pornography.**

I cried, held baby June, and allowed myself to get lost in my own misery. My thoughts raced feverishly. This photo incident coupled with the panties-in-the-briefcase incident seemed to suggest that Joe really did have a sexual screw loose. But now with the baby I was no longer working full-time. I ran my own grant-writing business from home and made great money for a second income, but I knew I could not support my baby and myself on my income. Joe knew that, too. Joe would deny everything, and I would look like the bad guy. I stayed in the marriage and kept my mouth shut.

Then, thankfully, the clues slowed down for a while, and I thought the past was just bad memories. We had worked so hard and jumped through so many hoops to adopt our sweet baby, June. Just a few months earlier we'd brought her home from the hospital when she was just one day old! We were exhausted from the grueling screening and approval process of adoption through a Christian adoption agency in north Seattle. After months of waiting and praying, beautiful newborn June came to us! We were delirious with happiness! Finally, after months of fertility testing and trying to conceive (we even used a turkey baster to insert Joe's sperm high into my vagina in hopes of becoming pregnant!) we had a baby daughter! But, the simple truth was that Joe and I rarely had sex, and, I, now in my mid-30s, had endometriosis, which made it all the more difficult to conceive.

I felt extremely betrayed, insecure, and very alone! I had planned on staying married to Joe forever, and now that we had a sweet baby daughter, I thought our family bond was solidified. Still, we had no sexual relationship. Before bringing children into our family I wanted Joe and I to have a better sex life, and Joe even promised to work on improving our sex life as we raised children, but it was a hollow promise. He didn't mean it, or he just couldn't. Just like he didn't mean it all the other times he'd said it during our marriage. What should I do? Sickened and haunted by the knowledge that Joe was "weird" sexually, I decided to dismiss it all—the pictures, the record cover, and the panties in the briefcase. After all, no one was getting hurt, right? Just me. It was okay because *I* could handle this. I was strong and had been hurt before. I was damaged. I knew from personal experience that damaged people are survivors—despite the damage. Maybe I really was overreacting. Joe was a good man, wasn't he? The fear of leaving him and starting out on my own paralyzed me. So I let the knot in my stomach get a little harder and decided to "shut up" like Joe asked me to.

We went on to adopt another baby girl, Ally, just 16 months younger than June. I'd seen no other indications of Joe's weird sexual manifestations. There were no more unaccounted-for long distance phone calls, no photos of pre-teen girls, no panties in briefcases, and no sexually suggestive album covers hidden under the driver's seat in the car. I lulled myself into a false sense of well being and told myself, *Sure Joe had a few weird quirks, but everyone did—so it was okay!* Our life together seemed really good except for the total lack of a sexual relationship. Although I would discuss our non-existent sex life with Joe every so often, I eventually gave up and decided not to keep knocking on unanswered doors. Little did I know that after Ally was brought into the house Joe groomed her for fulfillment of his sexual fantasies.

Another clue to Joe's pedophilia was how he interacted with our young daughters. When June and Ally were toddlers and preschoolers, Joe behaved as if he were a child himself! And to make matters worse he undermined my authority with our daughters and often left all parenting to me. I was the one who sent them to the time-out chair, told them "NO," and patiently taught them how to behave. **Clue number nine was the fact that Joe undermined me as a parent and tried to be a peer or best friend with our daughters.**

When Ally, was six, Joe began looking at Sunday's child in the newspaper and wanted to have a foster child. He wanted to adopt another little girl. He said, "We have so much to offer, and wouldn't it be great for our girls to have a younger sister? Then, appealing to my do-gooder philosophy he continued, "We'd be providing a needy little girl with a family and home."

I balked then replied, "No, I don't think the time is right. I'm not ready to do this now."

June and Ally seemed happy, and our family life was good. We traveled and had a gorgeous home in the country. I thought to myself, *Let's leave well enough alone.* Week after week Joe pushed the issue of adopting a foster child, but I continued to resist the idea. Somehow it just didn't seem right. When we considered bringing a foster child into our household I had no idea of the sexual relationship between Ally and Joe, but somehow our family seemed unsteady, unstable, and fragile. Even though I resisted, Joe forged ahead and called the number in the paper about two or three "Sunday's Children" featured in a Seattle newspaper. When he found one little girl about 3 years younger than Ally, he began speaking with the caseworker. Then, when I found out about him and Ally, I totally squashed the idea of bringing another little girl into our household. **Clue number ten was Joe wanting to bring another little *girl* into our household**. He made it clear that he was not interested in adopting a little boy.

Joe casually said, "We should adopt another little girl because we already have two daughters and it would be hard for a little boy to fit in."

Another clue to Joe's pedophilia was the fact that he liked to be around children too much and rarely hung out with adults at social gatherings and church. Joe was a popular Sunday school teacher and a church camp counselor. He obviously enjoyed playing with children and especially loved to play and cuddle with little girls. At first, I didn't attach any importance to his obvious enjoyment while around little girls. Other adults and I thought it was wonderful that he was "so great with children." I was disgusted when Joe sided with a camp counselor who was reprimanded for being found in the little girls' beach changing room. **Clue number eleven was Joe's choosing to be around children whenever possible and putting himself into leadership roles so he could be close to children and maintain a physical relationship with children.** He was always gently jostling, touching, or holding little girls on his lap.

Later when Ally was in kindergarten and June in first grade

we discussed a newspaper article. The story was about a child that was sexually abused. Joe called pedophiles "the scum of the earth."

Then, in the same breath, he muttered, "Our whole American culture is obsessed with sexual-abuse crap. It doesn't really physically hurt people. And besides, lots of kids lie about it anyway. In some cultures the father actually has sex with his young daughters to safely teach them how it's done."

I couldn't believe it! I argued his reasoning and replied, "That's ridiculous! Children are *hurt* by sexual abuse all the time. They are hurt both physically and mentally. It's something that children never get over. The results of sexual abuse are truly devastating. Children are haunted by sick sexual memories throughout their lives. They may never have normal relationships with the opposite sex. Many turn to drugs or alcohol or go on to abuse their own children. *And* all that stuff about other cultures is totally irrelevant, because we need to behave in appropriate ways in *our* culture. Your attitude is really weird!"

Then in anger he'd reply, "Geeze, Elly! You just don't get it, do you? I was just trying to be the devil's advocate. I was just trying to point out to you that there are other ways of looking at sexual abuse. I still think that Americans are overly obsessed with it and make a much bigger deal of it than is necessary. And remember, *you* can't be objective because of what the Abuser did to you."

His remarks bothered me, but maybe he was right. Maybe I was overly biased and couldn't be objective. Nevertheless, his words haunted me, and now I can look back and see that it was another red flag of abuse that I chose to ignore. **Clue number twelve was Joe's minimization of sexual abuse of children.**

Clue number thirteen was the fact that whenever I was gone from the household, Joe always gave the girls baths. Even when they were old enough to bathe themselves, he "helped them" but was actually helping himself by getting a sexual thrill just seeing his young daughters naked! I later found out that he washed their private parts with his fingers! During the nearly two years I'd known about Joe's abuse of Ally, I put the brakes on his scheme to bring a foster child, a little girl, into our dysfunctional household. I now realize that Joe wanted to groom another little girl to sexually abuse when he was through with Ally!

But the biggest clue to his sexual abuse was Ally's demeanor. I chose to view her reclusive nature and introverted behavior as simple shyness. The fact that she chose to stay home with Joe whenever I went out was another clue that something was wrong. Ally was very pensive, quiet, and analytical. As a toddler, she could sit for long periods of time by herself and study toys with moving parts to see how they worked. She clung to me when I held her. She was compliant, well mannered, and obviously out to please adults. **Clue number fourteen was Joe's manipulations to be alone with Ally.** He readily volunteered to do things with Ally like stay at home with her or take her for a short drive in the motor home.

Ally showed uncharacteristic anger towards Joe at her seventh birthday party. Joe seemed to side with one of Ally's birthday guests during a toss game. My quiet little Ally yelled and stomped up the stairs to her room. Joe followed her and they talked in hushed tones. Then Ally returned to the birthday game with tear-spattered cheeks and some grumpiness.

I asked Joe what the problem was and he just mumbled, "It's all worked out now. Just a case of birthday jealousy."

Again, the atmosphere felt strange. What was Joe *not* telling me? I tumbled the event over and over again in my head. Later it all made sense, of course. Ally thought *she* was Joe's "special girl," and when he showed favor to another little girl, Ally went uncharacteristically ballistic. I also found out that Joe had bribed her with the promise for a new doll to get her back to her party. **Clue number fifteen was the intense relationship between Ally and Joe.**

Bribing was Joe's middle name. He bribed us all with stuff. For the girls it was toys, clothes, candy, treats, and trips. For me it was jewelry, clothes, expensive home furnishings, and vacations. He even bribed himself! He often consoled himself with expensive, big-ticket items like new computers, new VCRs, laser-disc players, Polaroid cameras, a video camera, an expensive 35 mm camera, a huge truck, camper, sports car, big country home, fine crystal, china, silver, and furnishings. He always wanted more and more and more, so we took out a second mortgage and just barely made minimum payments on charge cards. He tried to salve his inner guilt with *Stuff* for everyone, including himself! Everyone outside our household thought we were living the American dream and that Joe magnanimously spoiled his young daughters and wife. We had lots of stuff, but the ugly roots of sexual abuse were quickly spreading under the surface of each of us. The façade of a dream life was fast eroding into a horrifying nightmare. **Clue number sixteen was Joe's constant desire to buy things, especially for Ally.**

Finally, clue number seventeen, was the fact that Joe preferred to masturbate rather than have sex with me.

He said, "It's just easier for me to masturbate. It's faster, I can fantasize, and I don't have to worry about not pleasing you or being impotent."

I found out later that he often fantasized about Ally or other young girls while masturbating. Sometimes he'd use a picture of Ally or another child to help him while masturbating.

I chose to minimize all the clues throughout my relationship with Joe. Even though I continued to pray daily, I was really simply going through the motions of being a "good" Christian.

I went to church, sang praise songs, and continued to stay in an unhealthy marriage. I knew God wanted me to fix my life, but I ignored his advice and instead chose to live in fear. Fear of starting over. Fear of poverty. Fear of people finding out what a sham our marriage was. Fear of letting the ugly secrets of our household out. Fear of what others would think. Fear of failure. Fear of doing what was right. Fear of making a mistake. Fear of the unknown. Fear of Joe. Fear of divorce. Fear of being alone. Fear of rejection. Fear of people blaming me. I was just one big ole wad of fear. You name it, and I was afraid of it. I was afraid of it all—so I lived miserably in my house I built with fears. Nevertheless, I struggled and persevered to preserve the image of a happy little family.

Prayer for Chapter Six

Dear God

I pray for women of all ages to listen to you and take your advice. Help us to make wise decisions and hold true to You in faith and trust, so we can fulfill the unique purpose we each have. Help me deal with the shock and the reality of discovering the truth about Joe and his sexual past. I feel like I was married to a sexual deviant—a monster—someone I did not know. Help me to deal with the chilling truth of who this man is. Don't let me be manipulated by him. Help me to not go crazy as I try to understand why all this happened. Help me and other mothers and wives to deal with all the fear. Dear Father God, help me to help my daughter.

Amen

CHAPTER 7
THE TIP OF THE ICEBERG

If we deliberately keep onsinning after we have received the knowledge of the truth,no sacrifice for sins is left, (Romans 10:26)

Rock a bye Baby on the treetop,
When the wind blows the cradle will rock.
When the bough breaks, the cradle will fall,
Down will come Baby, cradle, and all.

Unfortunately, Joe's confession was the tip of a very large jagged iceberg. His actions left a cold imprint in the hearts of all he touched. Over the years, he established a pattern victimizing more than one innocent victim solely to satisfy his sexual appetite. As more and more information became available, a clear pattern of sexual abuse unfolded which spanned a period of decades. All the pieces started fitting together, like a jagged jigsaw puzzle. One by one, the twisted little pieces fit together making a puzzle of the typical sexual pattern of a pedophile. His confession to CPS opened the door to a very well-maintained dark secret that spanned decades of his life.

In his initial report to CPS he confessed to only one sexual episode with Ally during which he stated he touched her and made her touch him. Through Ally's revelations over the next few months, it was apparent that the sexual abuse could have started when Ally was a preschooler of just four years old. Joe had probably fondled her when he changed her diapers, gave her baths, and napped with her. When I was away from our home, Joe heightened his sexual bond with Ally as he watched pornographic videos with her. Sometimes, he got a thrill by doing something sexual with her when I was home, but in a different room or outdoors! He became addicted to pornography on the Internet, and frequently viewed pornographic pictures with Ally. He repeatedly "played" with her in our bed and "tickled" her. He engaged her in oral sex. He rubbed her with olive oil. Why olive oil? He constantly fantasized about her and got sexual thrills from her when she wore skimpy summer clothing like shorts or a bathing suit or when she merely touched him. He made her dance for him in special sexy outfits! He loved to wrestle with her in bed and got sexual pleasure when she brushed against him. He took her to our bed to play the "tickle game." He took Polaroid pictures of her naked. He'd use these pictures at a later time to masturbate. He'd take her for short little afternoon trips in the family motor home. Then he'd park the motor home in a grocery store parking lot, draw the blinds, take pictures of her, and have his way with her. He kept his promises and bought her toys, clothes, and candy. He made her feel special because of their special times alone. Yuk! Yuk! Yuk!

His cycle of abuse continued for years with Ally. Joe later told me that after each time he vowed he'd never do it again, but, instead each time he became more tantalized and addicted so the abuse became more frequent and more complex. He found himself constantly fantasizing about Ally and sex. He could hardly wait for me to run into town on an errand or be outside gardening. He became more and more bold and daring with each sexual encounter with Ally.

I later found out that Joe's sexual problems started long before I met him. I was amazed and flabbergasted as the truth about Joe's sexual background was revealed. Joe remembers he was sexually abused when he was a child, but doesn't remember the details of who abused him. When he was a young man of twenty, Joe molested his younger sister, Gracie, when she was a teenager.

Then Joe's younger sister, Gracie, started college, and Joe started dating some of her friends. Gracie was one of my best friends in college, so in my sophomore year, I went out on a blind date with Gracie's brother, Joe. Joe and I became "steadies." Every weekend he would make the two-to-three hour trip up north to see me. During this time, I fulfilled Joe's sexual fantasies. I was nearly six years younger than Joe was, so at 19 or 20 he deemed me a great sexual partner. Of course, I did not know he was a pedophile, so the fact that he was 26 and I 20 didn't seem to be a problem.

Then Joe and I married when I was twenty. However, not long after taking our wedding vows, we stopped having much sex. In fact, our sexual relationship dwindled to the point of non-existence! I was shocked and dismayed! I couldn't figure it out. Why did our sexual relationship come to a screeching halt? During counseling, the counselors pieced the puzzle together for me. When I married Joe I became his WIFE—not a young girl. Furthermore, when I turned 21 and was no longer a child, he abruptly stopped having sex with me. Throughout most of our marriage we had very little sex, and when we did, Joe was detached and mechanical. I'd always wondered what went wrong sexually between us. We'd sought counseling after 10 years of marriage, and he vowed to work on improving our sex life, but never followed through with it. He liked to cuddle with me and seemed to be a wonderful partner otherwise, so I reluctantly accepted our sexless marriage. As the years went on, I got used to a no-sex marriage and concentrated on our children and my work.

In his late 30s and early 40s, Joe began to develop relationships with young neighborhood children. On summer evenings he regularly wrestled with two prepubescent neighbor girls on our front lawn. Neighbors and other adults just thought Joe had broken out of his shell and was experiencing a "mid-life crisis." Suddenly everyone thought Joe was great with children. Previously, in his 20s and early 30s, he hated kids and kept away from them. But, now he'd often invite neighborhood girls, whom he used to call "no-good, brattish kids," to go in our hot tub where he would goof off, joke, and playfully jostle them. It disturbed me that Joe was acting like a playmate of these girls.

About this same time (in his late 30s) he became gaga over my sister's daughter, aged ten. Previously he wanted nothing to do with my niece and was annoyed when I bought her gifts for Christmas and birthdays. Suddenly, Joe began wrestling with my niece and spoiling her with expensive presents. My sweet niece posed for him as he took photographs. Even though she was fully clothed there was an eerie sexual aura to her poses as she adoringly gazed into the lens of Joe's camera.

In his late 30s and early 40s, Joe taught Sunday school and was a camp counselor at a summer church camp for young children. I, too, was a camp counselor. I was uncomfortable when Joe held 7-year-old girls on his lap. Joe seemed to enjoy the little girls on his lap too much. During summer camp, another counselor was reprimanded for his behavior with seven-, eight-, and nine year-old girls. Joe felt sorry for the man and spoke on his behalf, even though everyone else felt the reprimand was just. Then, finally after months of bamboozling social workers, pastors, friends, and me, Joe had his own daughters to fulfill his sexual fantasies. Joe was in his early 40s when June and Ally entered his life.

I was totally amazed and shocked by Joe's past! I never dreamed that he got sexual thrills from my nieces or daughters or had a veritable history of sexual problems. There are probably countless other ways he fulfilled his sexual needs. He was so agitated and worried about the law officials' threat to confiscate our home computer that he spent hours dumping files of pornographic information that I never knew existed. Joe had worked very hard to maintain a façade of an intelligent man who was "great with kids."

How he became a pedophile is unclear. By his own admission, Joe was abused when he was a young boy. Joe was a typical child abuser who felt very guilty after each encounter but was unable to stop the cycle of abuse. With each subsequent encounter with Ally, Joe's abuse took on a new depth of psychological abuse fraught with bold and daring sexual acts. He felt somewhat guilty in the beginning, but the strong addictive drive for his sexual gratification won out each time. As time went on he had no conscience at all for what he did to Ally. He came to see Ally as a sexual instrument only — not a wonderful little girl. Sadly, Ally was solely a means to his sexual gratification — not a daughter to be loved and cherished. During Joe's treatment, pfismographs, sexual arousal tests, revealed that Joe was indeed sexually attracted to young girls and teenage girls. Women his own age or adult women were disgusting to him sexually.

After one of these sexual arousal tests, I was shocked when Joe said to me, "Can you imagine me being attracted to a woman in her fifties? Ugh!"

Every day he spent hours and hours gratifying his addiction for Internet pornography. Gradually, Joe's twisted sexual needs devastated our family, ruined our marriage, and nearly destroyed my beautiful daughter, Ally.

Prayer for Chapter Seven

Dear God,

Today I ask you to comfort me and other mothers as they learn the absolute truths about their husbands who have sexually abused their daughters. I ask you to help me understand how Joe and other sexual abusers can take advantage of beautiful innocent children solely for their own sexual satisfaction. Help me also to deal with the shame, the anger, and the shock of the aftermath of sexual abuse. Mostly, though, please help my little daughter to be brave and truthful, and let Ally know that she is loved by You, me, and so many others. Let her have hope. Help her to deal with the abuse so she can be happy.

Amen

CHAPTER 8
THE COUNSELORS

Plans fail for lack of counsel, but with many advisors they succeed. (Proverbs 15:22)

Little drops of water
Little grains of sand
Make the mighty ocean
And the pleasant land

My dysfunctional family was a real boon to the counseling business. After my initial three sessions with Mr. Bueler, I did not get further counseling for about a year until after both Ally and June, received counseling. I thought I could tough it out. Anyway, why did I need counseling? I was an adult, and the abuse hadn't happened to me. Besides I needed to concentrate on my daughters. I was fine. Right? But I was wrong. I was not fine, and I needed counseling just as much as my daughters, even though I had participated in a support group of adult survivors of sexual abuse several years earlier.

Long before I knew about Joe's abuse on Ally, I began having flashbacks of the Abuser sexually abusing me. When my own daughters, Ally and June, were just one and two years old, I would suddenly and inexplicably weep as I held them or changed their diapers. I soon realized the meaning of these heartfelt tears. I was remembering back to my own childhood of how young, small, and trusting I was when I was two or three, the age my abuse began. I'd never dealt with the issues of my own sexual abuse. Out of love for my daughters, I sought help. After all, they couldn't see me cry when I held them or changed them. After many phone calls I soon found the help I needed.

Every Thursday for about three months I participated in a support group of adult women who were survivors of child sexual abuse. The group was offered through the county in which I lived, and the facilitators of the program were empathetic and helpful. I was one of eight women who shared their sad past of sexual abuse.

Years later during Joe's participation in his sexual abuse program, I discovered some horrific news. While I was off to my Thursday night support group to deal with issues of the Abuser sexually abusing me, my husband was home sexually abusing Ally!

Now, soon after the CPS report was made, Joe was immersed in intensive treatment with a community-based sexual-offender program while Ally, June, and I sought counseling to deal with our emotional turmoil caused by Joe's sexual abuse of Ally.

Ally's counselor, Sammi, helped Ally deal with the reality of what Joe did. With religious faith, Sammi's help, and the support of family and friends, Ally was able to extricate herself from Joe's gripping and manipulative hold. Eventually, she was able to develop a healthy self-esteem and separate from the sexual identity she formed throughout her sexual relationship with Joe. Sammi also helped Ally deal with fears, anger, and stress. I knew Ally was dealing with these issues in her sleep, because I could hear her toss and turn as she slept and banged into the wall separating our bedrooms.

Occasionally Ally fell out of bed. She often complained of having nightmares in which some scary person or being was after her. In her dreams she would be terrified, never knowing whether she was actually caught or not. To help her get through the night, I gave her Timmy, my childhood teddy bear. I also gave her a satiny robe of mine so she would feel close to me after she got to sleep. Often I would snuggle with her to get her relaxed enough to sleep. Throughout this time, Ally kept up her grades in school and rarely received any grade less than an A. It was important for Ally to keep her self-esteem high and not let Joe's actions of the past affect her daily life. Ally's anger grew into a steadfast refusal to forgive. She wielded her unforgiving sword with pride and strength as she worked through the grueling counseling sessions. Bit by bit, a strong, new child emerged from the smoldering ashes of sexual abuse.

Under the direction of Ally's counselor, Ally would write down bad thoughts or draw pictures on paper and then rip them up as a way of ridding herself of bad memories. Ally also made clay dolls and figures, which she kept in a box. When she was sad, Ally would pull one of these clay figures from the box and hold it in her hands. Then she would transfer the unpleasant thought to the clay figure and quickly return the figure to the box, again ridding herself of such thoughts. She rarely spoke about the abuse other than venting anger of the injustice that Joe's actions had inflicted upon her. Week by week a stronger, more self-assured child emerged. Before my very eyes Ally blossomed into a bubbly, chatty, giggly, and happy little girl.

Our family doctor and Ally's counselor gently reminded me that the effects of sexual abuse are long term, and that Ally would probably need counseling at various stages of her life — especially as she developed into a teenager and when flashbacks or nightmares of abuse occurred. Nevertheless, I was very pleased that, at least — for now, Ally was happy.

The counselors and I were uncertain whether Joe had molested June. Even though Joe steadfastly denied any abuse of June, I suspected him because he lied so easily. June, also an "A" student, had other issues related to the divorce. Unlike Ally, June still loved Joe and missed him dearly. She missed the money and all the material things it bought. She hated leaving the large country home, which she often referred to as her "castle home." June very publicly blamed Ally and me for the divorce and the huge changes in her life.

Often she would mutter, "Everything was *fine* before, now it's *all* ruined!"

The final blow came when I had to give our beautiful dog, Gillie, away to another family, because he could not adjust to living in a housing development. Gillie was a country dog, and when we moved from the secluded country home to a housing development, Gillie was terribly unhappy and could not be contained by a fence. June was furious! Unlike Ally, who was ecstatic to start a new life, June was angry and embittered, because she loved her old life and old lifestyle. June, a child taking medication for ADD, attention deficit disorder, had never liked changes and definitely preferred the familiar. So, under protest, June went to counseling to address anger issues and to determine whether Joe had sexually abused her.

We were never able to determine whether June suffered any sexual abuse, because she didn't fully cooperate with the counselor. June felt she was "just fine" and didn't need any help. She continued to be angry, but gradually adjusted to the changes in our lives. She became distrustful of men. After all, her Daddy was not who he appeared to be, and he deserted her, so all men became scum. Even our family dentist would no longer would treat her because he felt she did not like men, and he recommended a female dentist in town.

Within six months from the time Joe moved, the divorce from Joe was final, and I was dating a longtime friend,

Thomas, regularly. Thomas, too, was ending a long-time unhappy marriage. We found each other and helped each other through some very difficult months. I had known Thomas as a friend for years. I probably would not have dated for a long time if I'd not already known and trusted Thomas as a friend. Our friendship blossomed into romance, and soon Thomas was living with us.

June was jealous of Thomas, and out of frustration she spat, "You're stealing my mom away from me!"

Ally tried getting too close to Thomas by trying to snuggle with him or by wearing skimpy clothing around him. Thomas, a parent of two grown children, knew Ally's behavior was a result of her relationship with Joe. Thomas made her change her clothes into appropriate dress for a nine-year-old, and he did not allow any inappropriate snuggling.

Both Thomas and I went to counseling so we could get the tools to let go of our past, move ahead to the future, and be strong parents for June and Ally. My counseling included weekly group counseling with Lucy Moore, Joe's counselor who ran the community-based sexual-offender program. The weekly group sessions were on Thursday nights about an hour's drive from my home. These sessions were absolutely free to any women whose child was a victim of sexual abuse by a man participating in Lucy's treatment program. These sessions were horrible and wonderful at the same time. I was rocked by the reality of the truth. Each of us women was on a journey of recovery from the horrid atrocities of sexual abuse on our children. As Joe revealed more and more details through therapy, Lucy shared everything he did to Ally. Weekly, I sobbed and cried as the painful truths were paraded out. Goodbye naiveté!

The harsh realities of Joe's sexual abuse of sweet Ally was profound! I could no longer protect myself from the truth. As the walls of deceit and betrayal came tumbling down, I came to see Joe as a monster, a man I never knew—a man I chose to marry—a man I chose to adopt children with, a man who, because of my stupidity, had sexually abused my Ally. Yes, I blamed myself. Lucy made it perfectly clear that Joe had manipulated me just as he had Ally. Because of my previous abuse by the Abuser, I was like a big ole target waiting to be hit. Lucy further stated that pedophiles could pick me out of a crowd of 100 people to have a relationship with and ultimately abuse my children. This was due to the fact that I seem trusting and naïve and able to be manipulated and controlled. Also I had not received in-depth therapy to deal with my early childhood abuse. Sure enough, whenever I'd questioned Joe about inappropriate behavior with Ally or June, he stated, "You're just paranoid about sexual abuse because of what the Abuser did to you."

The most difficult group counseling session occurred on a Saturday morning in a huge conference room full of pedophiles and their spouses. During the forty-five minute drive to the Group Session, I shook with anxiety. I asked myself—why am I going to this? Lucy was adamant that I attend. She'd made a career out of counseling pedophiles and their spouses, so she must know what she was talking about. But still, what could I possibly gain by looking at, talking with, and listening to *pedophiles?* When I arrived in the parking lot, I sat in my car for a few minutes and composed myself. I mustered up my courage to get out of the car when I saw Joe pull into the parking lot, park his Mazda RX 7, and enter the building. I watched him and felt strange. Had I really been married to Joe for over 25 years? He looked like a total stranger.

I uttered a simple prayer. "Dear God, please help me through this and hold me close. Amen."

The room was full of about seventy pedophiles and their wives, girl friends, mothers, or grandmothers. I acknowledged several of the women from our weekly women's support group led by Lucy. We were all seated at tables of four, two pedophiles and two caregivers of abused victims. I'd been anxious about this event for weeks. It was supposed to be good for me, move me along in the healing process, and give me some understanding of pedophiles, but when I walked in the room I felt nauseous. At the table, I welled up with hatred and emotion just knowing that the two men at the table were pedophiles. I sat stiffly as hardness engulfed my face. At first I could not look at *them* as they spoke, but then my natural-born assertiveness kicked in, and with disgust and fire, I glared at *their* eyes. I was horrified as I listened to pedophiles reveal their dysfunctional lives as boys who were riddled with physical, emotional, and sexual abuse (which I can not disclose due to confidentiality). I listened to them express heartfelt remorse. Were they all liars and manipulators? Many wore rubber bands on their wrists, which I later discovered was a form of behavior modification. Every time the pedophile had sexual thoughts of a child he would snap it hard against his wrist. This was supposed to help the pedophile stop thinking about children sexually. Some pedophiles were just young men in their teens or early twenties, but most were 30 to 60 years old. Some looked like plump, safe Santa's—like Joe. Some were athletic. Some were grizzled and hard looking. One was a woman! Yuk! Just the thought of a woman sexually abusing a child was completely repugnant and horribly sad to me. How could she? Thankfully, I did not get seated with the lone she-wolf.

What was I doing here? I must have been insane to think this would somehow help me in my recovery. I spoke with Joe at a break, which was taboo. Somehow I was still in his hold. I hated myself for gravitating toward him, talking with him, and unconsciously seeking him out. Again, I was jolted by the stark reality of sexual abuse. My heart bled for the innocent victims as I realized that many of the children abused by these pedophiles would, in fact, become pedophiles sitting in a room much like this one 20 years from now. Sadly, I realized that children learn from *all* their life experiences, even the unpleasant ones. I was painfully aware that the cycle of sexual abuse could be broken only if victims speak out and then seek and get counseling to deal with the abuse. Unfortunately, I also knew sexual abuse continues throughout generations if help is not sought.

A chilling realization came to me as I sat, almost hypnotized, in the room full of known pedophiles. They looked like normal people, they spoke like normal people, but normal they were not! They were tricksters, wolves in sheep' clothing, and consummate con artists. Each pedophile knew that having sexual experiences with a child was wrong, but nevertheless, chose to engage in sexual acts with children. This pocket of pedophiles snatched the innocence from children with no thought whatsoever of the child. I thought about how selfish and totally self-centered these child abusers were. The fact that they could blend into society undetected, in some cases, for years (like Joe) was incredible. They wore their masks of loving daddy, uncle, grandpa, or brother. They hid under the façade of a trusting teacher, camp counselor, pastor, or Boy Scout leader. Some lurked around playgrounds, parks, or day camps to surreptitiously select an unsuspecting child to groom and eventually sexually abuse. Others, like Joe, simply used their own young children!

Totally drained, I left the three-hour event and wept the entire way home. I didn't really want to know that there were so many sexual offenders in our community. I didn't want to look these pedophiles in the eye. I didn't want to think of them as people. I wanted to think of them as dirty, filthy, lowlifes and scum-of-the-earth beings. I learned through their confessions that most were ashamed for their actions and that not a single pedophile there wanted to be a pedophile. Although I'm sure many of them will continue to commit sexual crimes with children, it's not the type of recognition they want. They want to remain anonymous and blend in with everyone else. None of them thought they'd be caught, and none of them said, "When I grow up, I want to become a pedophile!"

Even so, I questioned the effectiveness of community-based programs for sexual offenders. Shouldn't pedophiles be locked up to keep children safe? How can a long-term pedophile change and not endanger young children? I knew that for each pedophile seated at the tables, there were another ten or more closet pedophiles, who, at this very moment, were satisfying their sexual needs with children! I also knew that for every reported victim there were scores of other unknown victims these pedophiles had abused. When I arrived home I slumped into Thomas's strong and welcoming arms and wept.

Lucy suggested that I get an individual therapist, but continue attending her group therapy as well. We each vowed to respect each other's privacy and not divulge specifics of the information shared at these meetings, but one general characteristic flabbergasted me. I was astounded that most women were staying married to the abuser of their children! I could not understand this. How could they stay in a marriage with the person who sexually abused their own children? At least I eventually left. How could they ever trust or love their pedophiliac husbands? Sadly, though, many women could not break away, due to financial or emotional reasons. I knew they were afraid, because I, too, out of fear stayed with Joe two years after I knew about the abuse. Many of the women minimized their husbands' abuse or felt they could be a protector for their children. I didn't know whether to feel sorry for these women or admire them. Surely it must take incredible strength and courage to stay in a marriage with a man who sexually abused your young children. But for me there was no question. I could never trust Joe again, and I didn't want a future of wondering whether he was having sexual thoughts every time he was in the presence of our daughters. Not many women chose to divorce their husbands for a variety of reasons. I held a good job, unlike many of the women. I had the financial means to support my family, whereas the others did not. My financial independence and the support of friends gave me the means to sever the tie to Joe and begin a new life. Although I was angry with the women who stayed with their pedophile husbands, I wept for them because they couldn't escape. As I got to know the women in the support group better, though, I grew to admire some of the women who chose to stay with their partners, because I knew they possessed a different kind of courage than I did. These women decided to give their husbands a second chance after they did prison time or time in a community-based sexual-offender program. They, unlike me, would have to be constantly vigilant when the family was reunited.

Eventually I no longer attended the support group meetings and sought individual therapy. My therapist was a young woman named Helen. She helped me deal with anger, betrayal, guilt, fear, and self-hatred. It was hard for me to let go of my self-blame. How could I have not known for so long? Then, when I did know, how could I have silenced the truth for nearly two years? I learned about the cycle of abuse and how devious and manipulative Joe was. But the best of it all, was the gradual disappearance of the hard, horrible knot inside my stomach. My daily tears and sobbing diminished. Even the daily thoughts of the abuse eventually declined. Helen told me to buy a whole box of paper clips and carry them around with me. Every time I thought about the abuse I took one paper clip and transferred it to another pocket or envelope. At the end of each day, I could see the number of paper clips decrease. By having something to do (transfer a paper clip from one location to another) every time I had a sad thought helped reduce the sad thoughts of the harsh realities and atrocities of Ally's abuse. Was this a coping strategy similar to the rubber bands on the wrists of the pedophiles?

Eventually, I, too, extricated myself from Joe and his grip. After more than a year of weekly counseling, Helen proclaimed me "normal" and ready to handle life on my own without counseling.

Counseling gave me the courage to write a letter to our relatives who wondered what had happened to cause us to get divorced. So, I sent copies of the following letter to my relatives. Even though most of them knew something about my divorce, I needed to let them know the reasons for the divorce. I shared the letter with Thomas and my counselors before I sent it off. Here's the letter.

May 1, 1998
Dear Mom,

Felony charges are being filed by the county prosecutor against Joe for several counts of sexual abuse/ and rape of a child. The victim is one of my daughters. That is the reason why I divorced Joe and why there is a restraining order against him having any contact with either of the girls. I will not tell you any specifics because I 'm sure you don't want to know. I will let you know that the abuse was deep rooted and lasted for several years. Joe has a serious problem with this sexual deviancy that stems back to way before he ever met me! He sure had me fooled!

I am telling you this so you know basically what has been going on in our lives. I was horrified to discover this, and the girls and I have had a really hard time picking up the pieces of our lives left in the wake of his lies, betrayal, and abuse. We are all in counseling—both girls go in weekly, and I go to individual therapy every other week and am part of a group of women whose sons, husbands, ex-husbands, and boyfriends have sexually abused their children. We were weary with all the running around as we worked really hard to put this stuff in our past and look toward the future. In the meantime we are trying to hold on to some semblance of normalcy with my job, the girl's music and drawing lessons, and some fun times together. I certainly would have never guessed our lives would have taken this turn and that I would be put in a position to protect the children from Joe.

As for Joe, his lawyer will work at getting the charges reduced—in any account his evaluation reflected that he is treatable—there is no cure: only himself being able to learn to control his deviancy. So he probably won't serve prison time, but will be granted mandatory participation in a state-certified sexual-treatment program for at least three years.

Anyway, this is the reason I haven't been writing as much as usual or sharing happenings in our lives. Through the grace of God, we are healing to the point that we can tell you about this. Remember us in your prayers and thoughts. We still hurt and feel anger and betrayal, but we do see a light at the end of the tunnel.

Love, Elly

Prayer for Chapter Eight

Dear Lord,

Today I pray for comfort for Ally as she relives the abuse in order to start her healing. Help guide the counselors through Your love to bring peace and hope for a different future. Help me to be strong for my daughters and to deal with my past sexual abuse so that I, too, have a better future. Help all children as they progress through a similar process.
Amen

CHAPTER 9
ALLY'S CHRYSALIS

You will grieved but your grief will turn to joy. (John 16:20)

Out came the sun
And dried up all the rain
And the itsy, bitsy spider
Went up the spout again.

Ally's rediscovery of herself was a slow and painful process. I was amazed by the courage she displayed as she went through the process of interrogation by the county policewoman from the sexual abuse unit of the county police headquarters. King County's Police and Justice Center was a large modern complex, and the Rape and Sexual Crimes Unit was a large, bright office full of individual cubicles separated by small, neutral-colored partitions. Ally and I arrived at 10:00 a.m. on a sunny Wednesday in July for a scheduled appointment with Officer Ann, who was the epitome of efficiency and professionalism. She welcomed us warmly and thanked us for coming. After speaking with me about Joe's confession, Officer Ann led us to a children's interrogation room.

It never occurred to me that there would be a cozy *children's* interrogation room full of soft cushions, colorful toys, and child-sized furniture in the Rape and Sexual Crimes Unit of the county police headquarters. It was then I realized with profound sadness and stark realism that my daughter was one of many children who suffered some sort of abuse by others. Officer Ann insisted on speaking to Ally alone because my presence in the interrogation room during questioning might affect Ally's testimony. While I was still in the room Officer Ann attempted to put Ally at ease by asking her several simple questions about how old she was and what grade she was in at school. Then Officer Ann asked me to leave. She closed the door as I slowly walked outside.

Although the cheerful children's interrogation room had eight large glass panes on one side and a small glass window on the door, it felt like miles of steel separated Ally from me. Ally tearfully held out her hands toward me as she let go of me.

Ally's eyes locked on mine as I tenderly murmured, "You'll be fine, honey. I'll be right outside the door waiting for you. Be honest with Officer Ann because she is trying to help us."

Uncontrollable tears tumbled down my cheeks. If there was ever a time I wanted to be with Ally, it was then.

While Ally was with Officer Ann, my heart throbbed and my mind filled with the horrible reality of where we were and why we were there. My thoughts filled instantly with questions and harsh realities. I married a man who sexually abused by daughter. I should have known. How could I have unwittingly put Ally in harm's way? How deep was the abuse? How far had Joe gone? How many times did he sexually abuse Ally? How much did she remember? How old was Ally when this all began? Was she in great emotional pain now? Would Ally try to protect Joe? Silent tears rolled down my cheeks, as I was lost in morose thoughts.

Suddenly the doorknob turned. Ally and Officer Ann came out of the cozy brightly colored room. Officer Ann let Ally choose a stuffed animal from a pile of new stuffed toys. Ally chose a soft teddy bear and clutched it tightly throughout the 45-minute interview. She came out of the interrogation room holding two stuffed toys, her teddy bear and a Snuflleupagus for her sister. Her toy was missing an eye. She chose the one-eyed teddy bear, because it was damaged and needed to be loved—just like her. She flung into my arms as we both wept with relief.

Officer Ann said Ally had been rather quiet and didn't say much, because she didn't want to get her daddy in trouble. However, Ally did reveal enough to substantiate Joe's report to CPS. Officer Ann mentioned that perhaps through counseling Ally may remember more or share more of what happened later. If Ally remembered anything more the next several months, Officer Ann instructed me to call her. Armed with Officer Ann's business card and comforted by her hugs, Ally and I left. Whew! We just took one more step on the road to Ally's rediscovery of herself. Officer Ann kept in touch with us over the next few months. She informed me that since Joe had confessed to the abuse, the county prosecutor's office would charge him with sexual crimes, which would result in a felony conviction if he were found guilty.

A few days after our meeting with Officer Ann, a county doctor examined Ally. Although the medical team was very experienced with working with sexually abused children, the exam was thorough and invasive. The doctor gently used a camera to take vaginal pictures of Ally to determine whether Ally had any vaginal tears or physical injuries as a result of the Joe's sexual abuse. Experienced and weary, the doctor gently explained the procedures and the reasons for the exam. Thankfully the results of the tests indicated that Ally did not have any vaginal or anal tears or any type of physical damage. Whew! I can breathe again—I'm relieved that Joe did not leave any apparent physical injuries to Ally's body. I offer a silent prayer of thanks to God. Perhaps Joe did not penetrate her with his penis.

Officer Ann contacted us four months later. The prosecutor's office was getting their case together for court and wanted us to come in. She asked us if we knew anything more about Joe's sexual abuse of Ally. Ally was more frank with Officer Ann this time. Through her individual counseling, Ally knew she did not need to protect Joe any longer, so she told Officer Ann everything she could remember. Her testimony did make the case somewhat stronger, however the most critical piece of evidence was the fact that Joe had, in fact, confessed to sexually abusing Ally. I could only attest to things Ally told me about the abuse, but I was shocked as more truth unfolded. I did not know the sexual predator side of Joe, even though I'd been married to him for more than 25 years. I was astounded at the depth of his manipulation of Ally and the boldness of his numerous sexual acts with her.

Nonetheless Ally blossomed! She became her chatty self once again, and played with classmates her own age. She smiled and giggled frequently, and through continued counseling she dealt with her emotions and painful withdrawal from Joe's grip. She sadly realized that Joe did not love her and had selfishly used her to please himself. Like most children, Ally missed all the toys, gifts, and "stuff" that Joe gave her in exchange for sexual favors. New toys and gifts were minimal for awhile as I struggled to make ends meet financially.

When we moved from the country house, Ally helped me throw the mattress from the bed Joe and I shared, off a second story porch. Shockingly, Joe had several sexual encounters with Ally on that same mattress! Ally squealed with therapeutic delight as we heaved the bulky mattress over the porch and heard it plop onto the ground below. We then took it to the county dump. One of the best balms for Ally was moving away from the country home riddled with sexual memories of things Joe had done to her. The barn, our bedroom, her bedroom, the den, the living room, and the motor home were all places that triggered sexual memories of what Joe did to Ally. These places caused dizzy, sexual flashbacks to replay in Ally's mind. I thanked God for letting Ally, June, and I start life over together in a new home, untainted and free of sad sexual memories.

I felt wonderful throughout Ally's chrysalis. Daily she improved. Although she suffered mood swings at the beginning of her counseling, she eventually became happy and content on a regular basis. She was angry with Joe and still (even five years later) wrestled with forgiving him. Ally truly wanted to forgive Joe but couldn't. I understood her reluctance. She felt if she forgave him that she would somehow be showing approval of what he did to her.

Eventually Ally's counseling ended, but her counselor did caution me that Ally might need future counseling, especially as she approached puberty and her teenage years. It was then I realized that Ally could heal and lead a good life, but the sexual abuse had left scars which could fester and become open wounds at particularly vulnerable times in her life.

Prayer for Chapter Nine

Dear Heavenly Father,

Today I come to you to a prayer for joy. I thank You so much for the healing of my daughter. I pray that other children, too, can feel joy and happiness and understand that sexual abuse is in no way their fault. Help me and other parents to keep a vigilant eye on these young victims of sexual abuse so that they continue to heal.
Amen

CHAPTER 10
A NEW MAN!

Love does not delight in evil but rejoices with the truth. It always protects, always trusts, always hopes, always perseveres. (I Corinthians 13:6-7)

Roses are red,
Violets are blue,
Sugar is sweet,
And so are you

The time was wrong, and I didn't feel like being loved by anyone. I was trying to let go of Joe and all the baggage from that relationship when Thomas waltzed into my life.

Okay, I'll admit it. I didn't really trust men and was angry with every man in existence. What good were they anyway? After all, both the Abuser and soon-to-be-ex-husband were men and, more importantly, pedophiles. And both caused me staggering pain through their manipulations of my trust and love. So, just to be safe and preserve my sanity and well being, I'd not jeopardize the progress I'd made by loving someone again. I decided that I could get along just fine without men. Why should I go to all the trouble it takes to form a meaningful relationship with a man when he'd end up betraying me anyway? I didn't want my daughters or me to get hurt all over again, and besides, I didn't really have the energy to put into another relationship. I was using every ounce of my resolve to help my daughters and me go through all the machinations with the legal system and the healing process with counselors. I knew that taking care of my daughters and me required most of my emotional strength. How could I have enough of myself left to become involved with a man?

Thomas and I were co-workers for three years and had developed a wonderful friendship. I grew to trust him as a friend long before my life turned topsy-turvy. We shared family news about our children, parents, siblings, and his grandson. As time went on, we shared personal thoughts about politics, religion, and our jobs. I began to tease him in a good-natured way, and we became pals who laughed together and enjoyed each other's company. When my marriage fell apart, Thomas was there as a true friend to help my daughters and me. He and other friends and co-workers helped us move all our belongings to our new home, and Thomas listened to me as I shared the hectic happenings in my life.

He, too, was getting out of a long, unhappy marriage. Eventually Thomas's kindness, friendship, and genuine affection grew into trust. At first I was afraid of trusting Thomas, but his genuine warmth, love, and kindness won me over. So in the midst of my tumultuous life, we began dating.

Thomas and I continued to be great friends as our romance blossomed. Before I knew it, our relationship became intense as we fed ourselves on genuine affection. Co-workers, acquaintances, and members of our families gossiped about us, and others even sneered at us.

We soon found out that we were fodder for the local gossip

mill in our small town. The fact that we were teachers and well known by parents and co-workers coupled with the fact that we were divorcing our spouses and dating each other, proved to be juicy gossip for several months. While shopping in the local grocery store, acquaintances shunned us by ignoring us, pointing at us, or averting their eyes. Some people had the gall to look right past us when we spoke to them, and I naively wondered why they cared. Didn't they have lives of their own to worry about? It was as if they, every divorced man and woman in our community, took out their feelings of guilt, shame, and betrayal on Thomas and me. Devastated by his grown children's reaction to his divorce and his new relationship with me, Thomas cried. My arms encircled him as his tears fell. Our emotions ran high as Thomas and I plodded along through the countless counseling sessions that permeated our daily lives. We endured excruciating emotional pain as we laboriously worked on putting our previous marriages in the past.

Then I began to worry that we were just holding each other together to support ourselves during and after our divorces, and after our troubles were over our relationship would end. I was afraid Thomas would hurt me like the Abuser and Joe did, so I expected pain, rejection, and betrayal. I began to taste the old fears—the old familiar fears that left me with a dry throat and a pounding heart. But Thomas's love remained constant and patient, even though I was afraid to totally let myself love and trust him. I was afraid to let my guard down. I thought for sure I'd spoil it all.

Even my counselors cautioned me about having a relationship with a new man. They asked me, "Are you ready for this? Are you sure Thomas is not a pedophile? Maybe he's just like Joe? You are vulnerable now. Does he want a relationship with you *or* your daughters? Why don't you play the field and date other men?"

I became suspicious and watched Thomas like a hawk. He

HUSH, HUSH, LITTLE BABY

did enjoy children, but I noticed that he wanted to spend the majority of his time with me, not my children. The more I shared about Thomas with counselors the more they liked Thomas, and eventually, they encouraged me to nurture our relationship. Our relationship grew stronger as we tackled each hurdle, and we eventually formed a sweet, intense bond unlike any I'd known since my daughters' existence or the wonderful pre-sex relationship with my Abuser. Thomas and I had the strength and courage to heal because we knew we had a future together. We wanted to be whole again and have a second chance at happiness through a marriage built on true love and respect.

After dating for about a year, Thomas and I got married. My wedding to Thomas was totally different from my wedding to Joe. Instead of dark doubts nagging at me, I felt like I was coming home to a place I was supposed to be all along. We wed in my house and invited only nineteen guests: family and close friends. My daughter's piano teacher played beautiful romantic music on our piano, and my dear friend, Elaine, sang pure sweet love songs. June and Ally wore a crown of silk flowers and were flower girls, dressed in white, flouncy dresses. The wedding celebration was marred only by the lack of Thomas's wonderful grown daughter, who refused to attend. I even wrote this love poem from my heart that I read to Thomas during our wedding ceremony:

OUR WEDDING
For Thomas

From the heavens high above
On this day HE shares His love
In all our hearts, let us rejoice
Feel HIS happiness and
Hear HIS voice.
My love for you will not waiver, wither, or wane

I'll comfort you through stress, strife, and strain
Today I become your wife
as we begin anew in life.

Together a strong, sweet home we'll make
A place for our families to partake
A place where we'll laugh, cry, listen, and smile
Yes, my dear, our union will be worth the while.

We'll watch our children and children's children grow
In our hearts and in our souls this we'll surely know
That you and I, we've spread our love
Nurtured by the Lord from above.

You've carved a place deep in my heart
a forever place, which will never depart.
These words of old—tried yet true
Still say it best, my dear, I love you!

Love, Elly
8/14/98

    I'm so glad I married Thomas. Otherwise, I would have constructed an impenetrable shield over my heart so tough that no man could have ever softened it. I know I would've become a bitter, unhappy woman who despised all men, just like many women in the support group who were betrayed by men. I would have raised my daughters to not trust or love anyone. Basically, my daughters and I would've formed an unhealthy, dysfunctional bond.

    Thomas grew to love June and Ally as daughters and, with their approval, adopted them. He parents June and Ally in a loving, yet firm way. Thankfully, he doesn't try to be their best friend, act their age, be physical with them, or bribe them with gifts or spoil them, like Joe did. Thomas is their daddy for the long haul, not for sexual gratification, like Joe.

At first, June resented my relationship with Thomas. Bitter tears seeped from her eyes as she shouted at Thomas, "You're stealing my mommy away from me. She loves you, not Ally and me!"

With a pang of guilt, I gently replied, "I love you and Ally, too. I've loved you for many years already, long before I even knew Thomas. The love I have for you and Ally is a different kind of love than the love I have for Thomas, but you need to understand that I love you very much. You also need to understand that I love Thomas, and he is a part of my life."

I gently stroked her hair, but for months June refused to soften. Eventually though, June realized that Thomas was not "stealing away all my love," and she began to like and trust Thomas. She was pleased that he wanted to adopt her, even though she was wary. June was fragile, because, after all, Joe, too, had adopted her but ended up relinquishing his parental rights. Would Thomas end up hurting her and leaving her, too?

Ally liked Thomas right away and was ready to have a real daddy in her life. She wanted a daddy to love her, help her, and treat her like a daughter, not a sexual toy. She was thrilled that Thomas adopted her, and she was proud to take Thomas's last name. Ally was receptive to Thomas's kindness, patience, and parenting. Naturally, she missed all the toys Joe used as bribes, but with age and maturity she realized that she paid Joe the high price of sexual favors for his "gifts."

Best of all was the change in our household. For the first time in our lives, we, my daughters and I, were part of a happy family. Little by little our rocky lives began to smooth out. We were wiser and smarter because of our pasts, and we were ready to forge ahead. Parenting was much easier for me because Thomas was a true partner in our marriage. Not only did we discuss everything from leaky faucets to the horrible realities of Joe's abuse on Ally, we were consistent with our parenting skills. I soon realized that Joe's spoiling of June and

Ally had undermined my authority, whereas Thomas's support helped Ally and June view Thomas and me as a parenting team. Like this passage from the Bible, Gary and I, too, worked as a strong duo filling in for each other as necessary.

"Two people can accomplish more than twice as much as one; they get a better return for their labor. If one person fails, the other can reach out and help. But people who are alone when they fall are in real trouble." (Ecclesiastes 4: 9-10, New Living Translation.)

Just two weeks after our wedding Joe had his day in court. Thomas was by my side as Joe's judgment day unfolded.

Prayer for Chapter 10

Dear Father God,

Help me and my young daughters to trust Thomas as a husband and father. Help us to trust his love for us. Also help me to not be fearful of the possibility of Thomas hurting me or my daughters in any way. Also help Thomas to take this healing, but battered wife and children under his wing of true love. Help this new family face the future with hope and true trust and faith in you. I also ask that this wonderful love between Thomas and me to last a very long time. Help other women in my situation to take a chance again and learn to love and trust another man. Help us to believe that all men are not pedophiles, and some are capable of being loving fathers and husbands.

Amen

CHAPTER 11
JUDGMENT DAY

Do not be afraid of any man, for judgment belongs to God.
(Deuteronomy 1:17)

All around the mulberry bush
The monkey chases the weasel
Five hands around and around
POP goes the weasel

Finally, on a beautiful sunny day in late August, more than a year after the CPS report was made; Joe had his day in court. Thomas accompanied me to the King County Court Building a large, modern structure, the same courthouse where my divorce had been finalized just ten months earlier. Someone from the district attorney's office led us to the courtroom and motioned us toward the plaintiff's bench. I looked around and tried to get comfortable in the formal room that exuded an efficient, official, and sterile ambiance. So, this is the place where attorneys would speak for Joe and Ally, and the judge would dole out a punishment for the crime of child molestation in the first degree. I did not frequent courtrooms. My only experiences in courtrooms were to serve on jury duty and adopt my infant daughters. Now, in less than a year, I was in court twice, once for the divorce and now this. I wanted the whole court business done with so I could get back to my "real" life and stuff all this in my memory of the past.

The room was cold, and the atmosphere was heavy despite the light-colored wood, the upholstered benches, and the soft-cream-colored walls. Why were other people there? Who were they? I wanted privacy and felt embarrassed to have strangers privy to my daughter's abuse. Within moments, however, their faces blurred and eventually blended in with the creamy walls and light-colored wood wainscoting. There was no jury, so the judge would listen to testimony and determine the sentence. I tried to remain composed and began to get sweaty and nervous. Judgment day really was here. Why was *I* here? I was not required to come. The judge had already read the letters, and she could make her ruling with or without me in court. I opted to come, however, so I could read my daughters' and my own carefully penned letters aloud in person and hear the judge make her ruling. Somehow it was important to me. I just knew I HAD to be there. I thought I'd be happy or, at least, relieved, but instead I felt anxious, sad, and awful. I thought my very soul was going to jump out of my skin and gaze down upon me as I sat there on the plaintiff's bench!

Suddenly Thomas and I heard a side door from the left of the courtroom open suddenly. It was the door by which prisoners entered the room from the county jail. Suddenly, everyone's head turned to watch the drama unfold. Sure enough, it was Joe. I was riveted like everyone else in the courtroom. I'd not seen him for months. I barely recognized the disheveled man in the neon-orange jumpsuit. He looked like a stranger, but he wasn't. He was the man who systematically, over a period of years, abused Ally and manipulated June and me. Two uniformed correctional officers escorted Joe to his bench on the opposite side of the courtroom. He was handcuffed and shuffled along with shackled feet. He was shaky and looked old, fat, and tired. But mostly, he looked scared and humiliated. He hung his head as he entered and briefly glanced my way. I was shocked. I felt sick to my stomach. This was all very real, and it was happening to me. It would be all right, and it would be over soon.

But things weren't really okay, were they? I became weak, and Thomas squeezed my hand as he told me to breathe so I wouldn't pass out. Damn, I wanted to be strong, not a weak, frail, little wimp! I had to pull myself together! I prayed for strength. Then I glanced at Joe again, and I saw him for what he really was: a 54-year-old pedophile. I was very suspicious of his appearance. Was it affected or genuine? Was the demeanor calculated by Joe or was he truly saddened and repentant? Was he still just "playing a game" and skillfully painting a sad, pitiful appearance for the outside world to see? Nevertheless, I was totally unprepared to see Joe as a prisoner—this man, who I slept next to for over 25 years, was in court awaiting judgment for the sexual abuse of our beautiful daughter, Ally. I shook off my momentary pity and shock, took in a deep breath, and focused on the judge as she entered the courtroom. Tension, sprinkled with abhorrence for Joe and pity for me, filled the courtroom as the charges were read, a felony count for two counts of child molestation in the first degree. He plead *Guilty* to both counts. The blurred faces of the strangers swung back and forth from Joe to me and finally fell on the judge.

I was anxious, scared, and embarrassed, but the reality of my purpose jolted me with strength. I was a woman on a mission. I was armed with three well-thought-out letters to the judge. My daughters and I each wrote a "Dear Judge" letter expressing our viewpoints on incarceration versus a community-based sexual treatment program, called SSOSA (Special Sexual Offender Sentencing Alternative) in legalese.

Lucy Moore, the counselor who coordinated and ran the local community-based program, convinced me that community-based sexual offender programs were much more effective than the treatment programs in prison, because convicted pedophiles who lived in the real world during treatment and were held accountable to the strict rules of sentencing were more apt to function in society and less likely to recommit sexual crimes. Lucy was a tough woman who ran a strict program in which pedophiles were held accountable for their actions. Lucy was smart, and years of working with pedophiles gave her the savvy to not be fooled by the manipulations, excuses, and whining of her clients. In other words, pedophiles in Lucy's program had to *talk the talk and walk the walk*.

Lucy told us that the judge would be more willing to grant Joe a SSOSA, Special Sexual Offender Sentencing Alternative, if Ally, June, and I wrote letters expressing our desires for Joe's sentencing. The judge received our letters in June, but it was nearly the end of August before his case was heard in court. When the judge asked me to read the letters, I squeezed Thomas's hand as I slowly and stiffly stood. Holding the letters in my shaking hand, I read loudly and clearly, but my voice cracked with emotion several times as I attempted to hold on to my dignity in court. When I felt like bursting into tears I took deep breaths and prayed. Here are the real letters Ally, June, and I wrote.

June 2, 1998

Dear Judge,

   I am very mad at Joe for what he did. I will never in my life forget how mean and selfish he was. I may (will?) never forgive him for what he did. I will always have a bad reputation for him. I feel very sorry for the kids that have gone through things like this.

I think that if Joe stays in program and truly understands what he did was wrong then he can learn to control himself. If Joe stays in program. I think he does not need to go to prison.

Sincerely,

Ally (age 10)
***

May 31, 1998
Dear Ms. Judge,

I would like it if my father could be put in a strong program unto which he could thus get better.

Child support is also an issue, for Mom (Elly R.) get's $773.00 a month. If my father (Joe) was to go to jail or prison for a not small amount of time he might lose his job. Which would result unto not more child support. Thus being $773.00 less each month, which she needs. This could mean less food, less money, not new clothes, and importantly a college education.

June (age 11)

***

June 2, 1998
Dear Judge,

The purposes of this letter is to introduce you to me and my family, share with you the effects that child abuse has had on my family, and to let you know how I want the offender, my ex-husband—Joe, to make restitution.

I was married to Joe for 26 years. I filed for divorce last summer as disclosures regarding sexual abuse were made by Joe and substantiated by my younger daughter, Ally. The divorce was finalized in November, 1997. I am an educated woman with a PhD in education from the University of Washington and, for the past 4 years, have taught full-time at a local Elementary School as a 1-6th grade reading and math teacher.

Ally, the victim and my younger daughter, is now 10 years old but was 9 at the time of disclosure. According to information that has trickled out over the past several months, Joe sexually abused Ally from the ages of 3-7 on a regular basis during times when my other daughter, June, and I were away from the home. Ally asked her father to stop at about the age of seven and he did. Ally subsequently became withdrawn and so unhappy that I knew something was amiss. When Joe made the disclosure to me I confirmed the abuse by speaking with Ally. I then called CPS and Joe made the actual report himself. I immediately got counseling arranged for my daughter.

Ally is in the gifted program at her school, takes piano lessons, loves to roller blade with me, and loves to read and play with her American Girl doll, Samantha! She is quiet by nature but the counseling she has received since the disclosure, has resulted in a wonderful blossoming for Ally. No longer withdrawn, she is friendly and openly happy now—as a mother I am so happy that the counseling has helped her reclaim some of her childhood. She is brave, strong, loving yet very sensitive and vulnerable. She is learning how to protect herself against potential pedophiles but sadly has a sexual education well beyond her young years. All's renaissance is due to therapy, a new start (we moved away from the home and environs where the abuse took place), faith, and lots of love and support from me, family and friends.

June is now 11 years old and, although she is not a direct victim of abuse, has had a horrible time adjusting to our new lives. She is on medication for attention deficit, but is very healthy and very active. She was close to her father and is now in counseling for abnormal fears (of bees, being alone in the shower—due to the fear of bugs coming at her from the showerhead) and intense anger resulting from the divorce and the change in lifestyle. June is also in the gifted class at school, loves reading, drawing, playing chess, being in charge, playing on playground rings, vegetable gardening, and collects fancy Barbie Dolls. She knows that her father sexually abused her sister, but finds it difficult to grasp the idea that it really happened and that somehow it isn't her daddy's fault.

Since the time of the initial disclosure, our lives have been totally overturned as we dealt with the stress, turmoil, betrayal and amazement by what had happened. Everyone we knew thought Joe was "great with kids" and a perfect father and husband. Our entire summer was spent in counseling sessions, interviews with police detectives, social workers, and lawyers. Ally had to go through an invasive physical examination. On top of all this, my daughters and I had to sell our family motor home, our big truck, and our country home on over two acres and find a new place to live. Even with child support our income decreased sharply—our combined income had been well over $100,000 per year—now my salary is about 45,000. I get about $800 per month in child support. So we had to find a smaller house—just about half the size of our previous house—in a development. I consider ourselves fortunate in that we found a new home close to my job for a monthly payment that I can afford. It has been difficult, especially for my older daughter—June, to accept the fact that things will not be the same monetarily again. My children had to leave their old friends and start at a new school—the school where I teach. I am proud of how well my daughters made the sacrifices and adjustments.

The biggest effect, however, has been the emotional roller coaster Ally, June, and I have been on over this past year. I am truly amazed at how this has devastated us and how difficult it has been to "get on" with our lives. Breaking the emotional tie to Joe was harder than I thought—therapy has helped me to see how he manipulated and used all of us to satisfy his sexual deviancy. I mistakenly thought that once I divorced him and got my children in a safe place that it would be over. Not so—I now realize that the pain we have suffered will never go away—it will diminish over the years, yet, there is nothing that can magically wipe away the deep sadness in our hearts. We can, however, pick up the pieces, learn from the past, and enjoy life with new and wiser eyes. With every new disclosure our wounds are opened again and yes, we bleed. We shed heartfelt tears to help wash away the pain as we deal with the stark reality of what Joe did to Ally. We talk to counselors and friends, pray, and listen to the experiences of others who have been through similar experiences. We also try to hold on to some semblance of normalcy as we face each new day. We do laundry, go to music and art lessons, attend school, go to work, watch movies and spend lots of time together. We've all certainly grown up very fast over the past year!

Now for Joe. Despite his sexual deviancy and sexual abuse on my daughter, Joe is hard working, intelligent, with a quick wit, dry sense of humor, and is a complex man. Unfortunately for us all, he succumbed to satisfying his sexual appetite and let his addiction to pornography totally take over his life. He became withdrawn as he spent hours hooked on the Internet pornography, took prescription anti-depressants, and sought counseling. He seemed to get caught up in a spiral of depression mixed with *bizarre sexual desires, yet portrayed a normal existence as a good father, husband, and employee.*

He pays child support every month in the amount of $778.00. Over and above that, he pays the co-pay for counseling costs in the amount of $58.00 per month and orthodontist costs of $50.00 per month. My other daughter will be in braces within a year, and there will be additional costs for her orthodontistry. He also contributes to Christmas and birthday gifts for my daughters.

He has been voluntarily enrolled in community sexual offender program and has had no contact with my daughters since last October. From my contact with Lucy Moore through the woman's group—Joe has expressed sincere remorse for his actions and wants to make restitution.

If at all possible, my daughters and I would like him to keep his current job so he can help continue to pay child support. I can, however, make ends meet should he lose his job as a result of being charged. It would be more difficult than it currently is to pay bills and put college costs away for each daughter. Since both girls are good academically, I would like them to have the opportunity to go to college— so I have $100 put away for each child from my paycheck every month. It would be difficult for me to continue this should he lose his job—but I'm sure I could cut down costs somewhere so I could continue to put money away for their education. So, do what you truly need to do—my daughters and I are well aware that Joe made some horrible choices, broke the law, and hurt us very deeply. He does need to make restitution and pay the price for his offense. We will manage financially with or without his help.

Also based on discussions with Lucy Moore, Joe is a good candidate for SOSA. If my daughters and I could be assured of the fact that Joe would be required to stay in Lucy's rigorous program for a minimum of 3-4 years and would not be allowed to have supervised visitations with my daughters until Lucy thought he was ready, we would be satisfied.

Joe cannot take away the pain he's caused Ally, June, and me, but with help and time, he can learn to control his behavior and deal with the profound effects of his abuse. His abuse took several forms including pornography through the Internet, pornographic videos, nude photography of my daughter, masturbation and oral sex with my daughter. I've learned that Joe has had a problem with sexual deviancy since he was a child. I realize that it will be difficult for him to control such deep- rooted problems. Since he truly does express remorse and wants to eventually see my daughters again he does have the "motivation" to sincerely work in a SSOSA program. He can continue to pay child support and help us financially as much as he can. But our greatest concern is that he learns to control his behavior so that he'll not offend again and hurt another child. I think that prison would not be as beneficial at this point as the requirement for Joe to participate in an approved sexual offender program.

Sincerely yours,

Elly R.

***

Without our letters Joe would indeed do hard time. Instead, he was sentenced to serve 89 months in a SSOSA. He was guilty of a felony for two counts of child molestation in the first degree. Should Joe not participate in the program he would then be sent to prison for any time left remaining on his sentence. Joe was ordered to register himself with local police as a sex offender. He was further ordered to have no contact with any minors unless accompanied by a "responsible adult who has knowledge of this conviction." The court findings stipulated that Joe could have no contact with Ally or June for life.

In addition to these court-mandated stipulations, Joe had to abide by the strict rules of the community-based sexual-offender program. He was required to undergo lie detector tests, personality tests, and sex testing, submit blood tests to test for HIV, undergo regular penile pfismograph testing (to determine whether he was sexually aroused by young girls), participate in several group-therapy sessions with Lucy Moore, and participate in individualized counseling sessions. Joe was not allowed to participate in any youth programs (like Sunday School teaching, camp counseling, or big-brother programs) or frequent places where children congregate (like malls, schools, beaches, arcades or fast-food places). He was ordered not to possess any pornographic information or frequent places where pornographic information was sold or viewed. While in the SSOSA program he was not allowed to watch suspenseful, cliffhanger movies or possess firearms. He could not leave the county without permission. He was required to be employed and pay for all counseling costs for himself and his victims as well as pay child support

Then it was over. Joe was led from the courtroom back to jail to prepare to go back to his home. Hand in hand, Thomas and I left and drove home. Joe got to go home and not serve any real hard time in prison. Even though Joe was sentenced to the 89 months in a SSOSA like I wanted, I resented the fact that he got to go home and begin his SSOSA program, and that was that. It was Thomas and I who would be there day to day for Ally and June. We were the ones to pick up the pieces of a broken little girl as she approached her teenage years. In short, Joe got to walk away. It was Thomas and I who had to deal with the fallout of his selfish sexual abuse of Ally. I just prayed and hoped that Lucy Moore was right—that by being sentenced to SSOSA, Joe would be less likely to sexually abuse other innocent little girls. It was already too late to prevent him from abusing Ally, so we were comforted by the thought that perhaps we somehow prevented the future abuse of another child.

Finally, another chapter in our saga ended with Joe's conviction. We hoped we did the right thing by recommending Joe for the community-based sexual-offender treatment program instead of prison. Now, new questions haunted us. Would serving a prison term be better for Joe than the SSOSA he ended up with? At least if he were in a prison program he would be locked up away from any young victims. Would Joe abide by the rules of the court and the program or would he secretly continue using pornography on the Internet? Would he seek out young girls for sexual arousal and satisfaction for the rest of his life? Would he maintain friendships with other men who were involved with kiddy pornography? Would he continue to get sexually aroused by memories of Ally and their sexual encounters? When he saw a little girl would he automatically get sexually aroused? Would he ever be normal sexually? What about after he served his sentence? Would he seek out another victim in a different town, county, or state? Would he attempt to seek out Ally after his sentence ended? Would Ally be all right as she became a pre-teen, teenager, and young woman? How would she interact with boys and men? Would her happiness and joy in life continue?

Prayer for Chapter Eleven

Dear Lord,

I know that eventually Joe will face judgment with you, but my daughters and I thank you for the justice today in court. I truly pray that Joe will take the SSOSA program seriously and will not sexually abuse other children in any way. I also pray that Ally has some feeling of justice so she can continue to heal and be happy. I pray that all children who are victims of sexual abuse experience some sort of justice for the horrible aspects of sexual abuse. Help us all to shed the heavy burden and long-lasting effects of sexual abuse.

Amen

CHAPTER 12
THE FALLOUT

Be joyful in hope, patience in affliction, faithful in prayer (Romans 12:12)

Ring around the rosies
A pocket full of posies
Ashes, Ashes,
We all fall down!

In the autumn days following Joe's sentencing, our lives changed as quickly as the leaves changed from green to gold. Ally, June, Thomas, and I worked hard at reconstructing our complex, fragmented lives by putting the past behind us with prayer, counseling, work, and each other. We went on with our daily lives as we dealt with the fallout of Joe's abuse on Ally. Even though Joe's extended family provided support for him, the girls and I were stunned by how Joe and his relatives handled his conviction.

Immediately following his conviction, Joe was angry and blamed me for his "felony" charge. He was not yet ready to take the blame or the consequences for his actions. Although he freely admitted to sexually abusing Ally, he felt that the *felony* charge was unfair and thought a misdemeanor charge was more appropriate. Because I initiated the call to CPS and encouraged Joe to make the report himself, he blamed me for the *felony* charge. Had he denied the charges and never admitted to CPS that he had, in fact, molested and sexually abused Ally, he could have been charged with a misdemeanor rather than a felony.

Joe's family rallied around him and swiftly and heartlessly severed the relationships with my daughters and me. Stung by the abrupt cut-off by Joe's relatives, I bewilderingly turned to Thomas and the girls. As I explained that Joe's relatives no longer wanted a relationship with them, June and Ally burst into hard, bitter tears. Ally and June could not fathom how their much-loved relatives could dump them so casually and callously. Couldn't they love Joe and still love young Ally and June? Apparently not. Our conversation went like this:

With tears streaming down her face, June indignantly queried, "Mom, how can they do that to us? I thought they loved Ally and me?"

I hugged June and then replied, "I thought they loved you, too, but apparently they just can't give their love to you girls *and* Joe. Remember that Joe is theirs. They feel their first allegiance is to Joe not to you girls."

Ally then added, "But they sent us lots of money for our birthdays and Christmas. They gave us lots of presents ever since we were babies. They must've loved us. Or...did they not love us deep down?" Her questioning eyes, glassy with tears, revealed that she knew the truth.

I wiped away her tears and answered back, "You know, I think you're right, Ally. They did not love you deep down. All the money and presents over the years did not express a true love for you. I am so sorry. This must hurt a lot. I am just as stunned as you. I didn't expect this to happen."

Tears then, finally, spilled from my eyes as I empathized

with June and Ally. In one swift phone call, Joe's relatives had casually cast them aside like an old pair of shoes that was no longer stylish. Just to make sure we understood the finality of their decision, his relatives sent the girls a letter in which they stated that "if either of them (June or Ally) were ever in any trouble of any kind they would, of course, help them out. If the girls ever needed any money, Ally and June could call on Joe's relatives. All June and Ally had to do was ask." Both June and Ally knew the hollow words of the letter were meant to assuage his relatives' own bitter guilt and make them feel less guilty for "dumping" June and Ally. Out of hurt and rejection, Ally and June vowed to never ask Joe's family for help. Their rejection was compounded by the fact that they were not related by "blood" to Joe's family. They wondered if his relatives would have discarded them so easily if they were the "real" children of Joe rather than "adopted" children.

Unwittingly June and Ally added another brick to their walls of distrust in an effort to preserve themselves. Through no fault of their own, their birth mothers chose to put them up for adoption as babies, then, their daddy sexually abused Ally and suddenly was their daddy no more, and now their beloved relatives dumped them. It was almost more than we could bear.

The severed relationship with Joe's relatives added more turbulence to our already fragile and stressed family. A shell hardened around us in an attempt to deal with the shock of the rejection by Joe's family, but we actually grew closer as a family. We felt terribly beat up by Joe, his relatives, and the court process, and even the "healing" process was rigorous and difficult. We knew if we didn't heal, Joe's abuse of Ally would continue to victimize us forever. So, we assumed a healthy attitude of, *If we can make it through this, we can make it through anything.* We prayed, cried, yelled out of frustration, and hugged each other often. Mostly, we just survived.

One night after work while preparing dinner with Thomas, I went to the silverware drawer and reached for a knife to butter bread. All the knives were in the dishwasher, and the silverware drawer was empty. I was exhausted from working on my job, counseling, parenting, and day-to-day existence. The frustration and stress of the last few months caught up with me. I grabbed the kitchen counter to steady myself.

I looked Thomas in the eyes, and tearfully wailed, "Now…there are *no* knives, *no* knives, *no* knives. Again, *no* knives. All I wanted was a knife, and they're all dirty. They are all in the damn dishwasher! There's not even one fucking clean knife in this house."

(All this from me, a woman who rarely used swear words!) I ran from the kitchen to my bed, leaving the staring blank eyes of my family behind. It was just too much. The "no knife" incident was the straw that broke my back. I unleashed months of tears as Thomas joined me and held my sobbing, wretched body in his arms.

Almost immediately after the sentencing, Joe lost his well-paying job with the aerospace company. He was embarrassed by his felony conviction, which he had to fess up to on job application forms, and he was forbidden to work at any job that even remotely pertained to children. His child support payments decreased, but he eventually got employment as a receptionist. He had to register with the local police office as a sex offender and could not live in any apartment complex or dwelling that housed children. In fact, he had to move several times because families with children moved in close to his apartment or condo. He missed his high paying salary, his work friends, and the prestige of a well-paying job. He begrudgingly adjusted to a less-prestigious job, a lower income, and no friends. He participated actively in the sexual-offender program according to his sentence, but viewed himself above the other sexual offenders in the program. He did not see himself as one of those "scumbags." He viewed himself as different because he was educated, intelligent, and just "a better class of people" than the other sexual offenders.

A few months after Thomas and I married, we asked Joe if he would relinquish his parental rights of Ally and June.

Joe seemed sorrowful about giving up his paternal rights of June, but bluntly blurted, "I have no feelings for Ally. I know that's something I'll have to work on in counseling. I just never bonded to her like I did to June. Make sure June understands that I'm giving up my parental rights only because I can never see her again. I don't want the girls to feel like I don't care."

Chills ran up and down my back when Joe said he had "no" feelings for Ally." For years she yielded to him and gave him everything he wanted sexually, yet Joe had *no* feelings for her. I was sickened by his words. He'd manipulated and used Ally for his own sexual gratification since she was a toddler! He did not see her as a wonderful child but a mere sexual object for his own fancy! It was then I realized that I did not know Joe at all. He was not the man he portrayed himself as or the man I believed him to be in my mind. How truly sad my previous life with him was. Like a dog shakes off water after a bath, I shook off past memories and present shivers. Now I was headed down a new road without Joe, his lies, his problems or his phony feelings.

Within a few days of our request, Joe gave up his parental rights of Ally and June. He consulted with Lucy Moore, the counselor who ran the community-based sexual offender program. Lucy encouraged Joe to relinquish his parental rights, because by doing so he would help Ally and June have a better family life. Joe also realized he would not be required to pay child support if he was no longer June's and Ally's legal parent. So within seven months of Joe's sentencing, Thomas became the legal father of June and Ally.

Over the next two years, we reeled from the changes in our

lives. First, Joe had made the CPS report, moved out, and was charged with a felony for sexual abuse of Ally. Next, Ally underwent a physical exam at a clinic to determine if Joe's sexual abuse damaged her physically, and Ally and I met with detectives from the Sexual Crimes Unit. Then, the girls and I moved, and Ally and June attended a new school. Joe and I filed for divorce. Thomas and I began dating, and he moved in with us. We all started counseling, and Thomas and I married. Joe was convicted, and his relatives severed their relationship with Ally, June, and me. Then Joe gave up his parental rights to Ally and June, and Thomas adopted Ally and June. Thankfully, the girls had a new extended family, and Thomas's mom became a new loving grandma to June and Ally. Like a loving mother hen, she took them under her wing as her own. After their initial shock to Thomas's divorce wore off, Thomas's son and daughter (from his previous marriage) came to accept my daughters and me and love us as family. As I got to know Thomas's children I grew to love them very much.

So, like a scratching dog gets used to fleas, we became accustomed to dealing with the many twists and turns of our careening lives. Change, in fact, became normal. Fortunately, the negative changes slid by us as the turbulent wind became a warm balmy breeze that swept us up and plunked us down in a new world of day-to-day happiness.

Prayer for Chapter Twelve

Dear God,

Today I pray for hope for Ally, June, Thomas, and me as we face our future. Now that all the legal actions, counseling, and dealing with authorities is over, help us to be whole and move on. Especially help Ally to forget the things Joe did to her and focus on today and tomorrow. I pray for all the families that are dealing with the reality of putting their lives back together. Finally, I thank you for Your love and patience with us all.

Amen

CHAPTER 13
LESSONS LEARNED

For the Lord gives wisdom and from his mouth come knowledge and understanding. He holds victory in store for the upright, he is a shield...to those whose walk is blameless. (Proverbs 2:6-7)

A dillar, a dollar,
A ten o'clock scholar,
What makes you come so soon?
You used to come
at ten o'clock,
But now you come at noon.

Like the tardy scholar, I, too, was late to learn my lessons, but learn them, I did! Throughout the whole horrid experience I begrudgingly learned some very important life lessons.

First, I learned not to give up on my faith. Right after I found out about Joe's sexual abuse of Ally, I felt wounded and hurt, and I let myself drown in psychic pain, which caused me to doubt my belief in God. I couldn't understand how or why

God let my family suffer the consequences of Joe's actions. I blamed God, my awesome, all-powerful God for not protecting my daughter. Why was a sweet innocent child, Ally, betrayed by her daddy? Wasn't it enough that the Abuser had sexually abused me? Why did God allow history to repeat itself and result in my daughter being abused by her daddy, my husband? Why? Why? Why? I blamed God since He surely could've prevented it all. I chose bitterness and prayed with a mean, hurt heart as I hurled nasty accusations at Him.

Then I directed my hatred to myself. I felt everything was my fault—if only I'd listened to my heart and not married Joe, if only I'd not let Joe manipulate us all, if I'd not agreed to adopt children with Joe, especially since I knew there was *something* wrong with him, if I'd only known about the abuse earlier, so it didn't go on for years, if I reported the abuse as soon as I discovered it. If—If—If! Surely God was punishing me, and I was totally unworthy—not deserving of anyone's love, especially God's. After months of wretchedness and misery I finally had enough bleak, dark, meaningless days. Miraculously, out of utter desperation, I returned to genuine prayer and prayed with utmost sincerity and let myself accept love from God and other caring people he put close to me. The heavy locked doors to my heart and soul burst open as sunlight entered my very being. **I learned to pray with intensity and sincerity**. I let go of my blame and anger toward God and myself. I gradually grew to trust in God. As the Bible states, "I waited patiently for the Lord to help me, and he turned to me and heard my cry. He lifted me out of the pit of despair, out of the mud and the mire. He set my feet on solid group and steadied me as I walked along." (Psalms 40:1-2, New Living Translation)

I learned to blame Joe for the things he needed to be blamed for. My family and I returned to church and allowed ourselves to heal. We became approachable, and we allowed friends and family to nurture and love us again.

Secondly, I began to share our experiences with others, including several close friends and my family. The amount of support, understanding, and love we received was amazing. My mother, brother, sister, aunts, uncles, and grandfather supported us with understanding words in letters and phone calls, but mostly they listened. Thomas's family provided wonderful support as well. When I needed $3500 for a rebuilt engine in my car (due to the hectic life immediately after the CPS report was made, I neglected to put oil in my car and its engine froze up while I was driving Ally to a counseling session), my understanding mom came through to lend me the money. Thomas's mother, too, was also a wonderful comfort to us. On mornings when I just couldn't contain pent up tears, coworkers cried with me and offered hugs, tissues, and comforting words. Longtime friends, who met me for lunches or suppers, listened and empathized with us as my family dealt with shock, betrayal, and sadness. When I couldn't talk to my extended family because I cried so easily, I wrote them letters. Sharing the nasty secret began to release my family and me from its tenacious talons.

Thirdly, I realized we all needed the help of professional counselors. As much as I wanted to take care of my family and our problems all by myself, I had to let go of fantasy and grasp reality. In other words, I had to grow up and let go of the twisted fantasy world I'd constructed for years. Nevertheless, I was terrified to leap ahead and hurl my daughters and myself onto the counseling couch. The very thought of sharing my family's ugly secret with total strangers, who would analyze it all and then spit out advice even though they didn't know anything about my family except what I told them, was abhorrent and scary. However, it was painfully clear that professional help was absolutely necessary for all of us. Counseling was very demanding, draining, and tough, but the more honest and courageous I was, the better I felt and the faster we all healed. I soon realized *I* was the key to unlocking my family's healing. I had to hold myself together for the sake of my family and myself, which meant I did not have the luxury of selfishness. Although living in a cesspool of pain, hatred, and resentment offered a certain amount of strange comfort, I could not allow my daughters or new husband to see me drown in a never-ending sea of bitterness and self-pity. I *had* to serve as a model and a survivor for my Ally and June so they, too, could heal.

I also learned the true meaning of forgiveness. First, I had to forgive myself, which sounds easy, but was, in fact, extraordinarily hard. I hated myself so much and often doubted whether my family could survive. Through, prayer, caring counselors, and the support of family and friends, I realized it was Joe who started all of this, and no matter how much he tried to blame me, I too, was a victim of his manipulations. Joe created this huge, awfully complex mess, and it was up to me to start and continue the cleaning-up process. As soon as I started forgiving myself I began to feel released as the hard knot in my stomach gradually softened. I tasted sweet freedom, and yes, some happiness and light began to slowly creep into my otherwise dull, dark world. Although I thought I'd never be able to forgive Joe, an absolutely incredible thing happened. I called Joe nearly five years later and forgave him. This sounds unbelievable, but I had to forgive so that he no longer had any control over me.

I shook and my voice quavered as I held the portable phone and muttered, "Joe, I don't know whether this is important to you or not, and I guess I don't really care, but I thought you'd like to know that I forgive you for what you did to Ally. But I will never, never think it was okay, what you did."

Silenced for several seconds, Joe then replied with slow measured words, "Well, thanks for letting me know. My counselor says people forgive for themselves, not to make anyone else feel better."

In my case, it was true. I did forgive Joe for my family's

sake. I knew it was the right thing to do, but I fought it for five years, and throughout the fight I let the issues of his abuse on Ally control me. Scenes passed through my mind every single day like a sad, never-ending movie, and thoughts of Joe's abuse of Ally continued to torment me and erode my soul. Five years of holding on to deep-seated pain had caused a continuous and insidious cycle of pain to run rampant deep within me. I finally realized I could forgive without ever forgetting. Again, this sounds trite, but *not* forgetting was extremely important to me. By *not* forgetting the abuse, I can remain vigilant and smart so my daughters will not be in jeopardy again. I will never trust Joe or believe him.

Five years later, Ally's was not yet able to forgive Joe, and this I understood. It's so much harder to forgive a daddy than a husband! I was not able to forgive the Abuser until 45 years later—long after he died. **There's nothing, NOTHING, more freeing than forgiveness**. Like a dog that vigorously shakes off water after a bath, I shook off the last remaining hold Joe had on me.

Suddenly at age fifteen, Ally asked for a face-to-face meeting with Joe so she could forgive him! I was in shock!

Ally explained it to me, "Mom, I want to forgive Joe. As I grow in my Christianity I know I am called on to forgive , so I don't carry resentment and a refusal to forgive forever. It will only fester inside of me. I'm ready. I have to do this."

I contacted Joe's sexual offender counselor, Lucy Moore, and presented Ally's request to her. She suggested that Ally do this via a video tape or telephone so that Ally would not have to see Joe face to face. Ally considered these options but chose to have a face-to-face meeting. So Thomas and I met with Lucy and Joe in a small conference room with about fifteen chairs in a circle in the middle of the room. This was the room used for group sessions. Ally sat in between Thomas and me on one side of the circle and Joe and Lucy sat on the other side.

Ally looked straight at Joe and began, "Joe, I just want you to know that I forgive you for what you did to me. I hope you, too, can find Jesus in your life. Jesus loves you. You need to give Him a chance."

Joe's face was flooded with tears as he sobbed, "I don't deserve your forgiveness. I am so sorry for what I did. I also want apologize to you, Elly, and to June for messing up our lives. I was very selfish."

Ally countered, "Joe, can you promise me that you will never do what you did to me to anyone else?"

Joe replied, "I wish I could promise that, but in program we are taught that we can't make promises like that. I can tell you that I will do everything I can so that it doesn't happen again."

During this whole time I was filled with pride for Ally. How could she at age fifteen forgive a father who sexually abused her? I knew it was because of the strength she drew from her Christian faith. I was still filled with distrust and disgust upon seeing Joe. I didn't believe his words or his tears. I do know that forgiveness is an amazing healing tool. I thank God for the courage he gave Ally and me to forgive Joe. I, too, was eventually able to forgive the Abuser for sexually abusing me, even though he'd been dead for years.

I also learned to follow my "gut" instincts whether they make sense to anyone else or not. The "gut" instinct is, in fact, God given, and I should not have ignored it. Regrettably, I learned this the hard way. Neither my children nor I would be in this intricate mess if only I'd followed my gut instincts from the beginning. When every muscle in my body told me not to do something, I did it anyway. I married Joe even though it didn't feel quite right, and lived with for years knowing that *something* was dreadfully wrong. Conversely, when a driving force told me to do something I ignored it! I remained with Joe for nearly two years after I discovered the abuse! Even though I confronted a fear of height by daringly leaping out of a plane at 13,000 feet at the Issaquah Skydiving

Center and by reaching the peak of Mt. Rainier at 14,410 feet, I didn't confront the real fears in my day-to-day life. I didn't follow my gut feelings. Instead I allowed myself to live with a man who distanced himself from me and refused to have an honest relationship with me. Out of fear I let myself stay in an unloving and unsatisfying relationship that was doomed to fail, and unfortunately, my daughters suffered the consequences of my actions.

Being part of a support group was even more essential than individual counseling. In the sad, and shocked faces of the hurt, distraught, and betrayed women, who were members of the support group, I saw mirror reflections of myself as we shared details of heinous sexual abuse on our children by our partners. We were comforted, however, by the sad fact that we were not alone in these very personal sexual abuse experiences. Many of the women, like me, had suffered sexual abuse themselves either through rape or sexual abuse as a child. We also went through similar emotions: **first**, the disbelief, shock, and minimalization of the abuse; **second**, the wanting to blame ourselves or our children rather than our partner, **third**, the pain and anger usually accompanied by sobbing and yelling; **fourth**, the craziness and insanity of how to make it through the day; **fifth**, realization that the abuse is *not* our fault but is, indeed, our partner's; **sixth,** the self-flagellation for not seeing the abuse sooner or reporting it sooner; **seventh**, the realization that the abuse is something that is never entirely over, but something over which we have the power and choice not to let consume our lives; **eighth**, the decision of whether to stay with our partners or divorce; and, **finally**, the realization we have to take care of ourselves and our children in order to move away from self-pity, remorse, and fantasy toward responsibility, empowerment, and reality.

I learned that justice in some form was essential for our deep-seated feelings of bitterness, betrayal, and resentment

to diminish. Justice took on many forms, including Joe's self-admission of the abuse, his being charged with a felony, the judge's guilty verdict, and his sentencing to years of mandatory participation in a community-based sexual offender program. Ally could begin her healing process knowing that I believed her and that the court believed her—it doled out major consequences to Joe for his abuse. We learned there is a very fine line between revenge and justice. There was a time when Joe begged me to hit him for what he did to Ally, and although I dearly wanted to smack him really hard, with pent-up anger and anguish, I innately knew that by punching him he would feel better and less guilty. The refusal to strike Joe was justice. Writing and then reading the "Dear Judge" letters in court was another form of justice. The fact that Joe is now a registered sex offender and cannot be around any children is also justice. The fact that Ally was courageous enough to tell the truth to police detectives made it possible for Joe not to abuse any other children—at least while he's in program. This, too, is a form of justice.

I became "smart" about pedophiles, their traits, their cycle of abuse, and their profiles. I learned that there are three classifications for sex offenders in Washington State. Level 3 sex offenders are the most dangerous type of sexual predator. They are at a high risk to re-offend and typically have one or more victims. Level 3s may not know their victim, and they usually deny or minimize their crime. Their crimes may involve violence. A Level 2 sex offender has a moderate risk of re-offending. They may have more than one victim and typically groom their victims. Level 2s typically use threats and often use their positions of trust to gain the confidence of a victim. They do not recognize the damage they've done to a victim. A Level 1 sex offender usually knows his/her victims. First-time sex offenders are typically classified as a Level 1 sex offender. A Level 1 offender is considered to be the least dangerous type of sexual offender, who commits sexual crimes with family members or someone he or she knows. Joe was classified as a Level 1 sexual offender, since this was his first reported offence, and Ally was someone he knew. Sadly, I learned that in my county alone there are more than 2,000 registered sex offenders! However, of these 2,000, three-fourths are Level 1 sex offenders.

I frequently do a computer search to find out how many registered sex offenders live within a five-mile radius of my home, and I inform my daughters. I learned that pedophiles are not cured—the best we can hope is for pedophiles not to act on their twisted sexual drives. Our school district does a great job informing us when a registered sex offender moves to our locale, but I also know there are many pedophiles who have not yet been caught, so I maintain vigilance. I think I could spot a pedophile by watching his interactions with children, but I take no chances. I no longer leave my daughters, now teenagers, alone with any adult unless I know the adult. Although my daughters have dubbed me as "overly protective," I am suspicious of adults in leadership positions who are too familiar with young girls. Male teachers, counselors, or church leaders who try to relate too personally with my daughters are suspect. Their actions often raise a red flag. I make sure my daughters are never alone with adults who jostle or hug children in a too familiar way. Adults who touch children frequently, are too popular with girls, or try to become overly friendly are also suspect. When an adult seems to want to spend time only with my daughters or children and not other adults, again, I am suspicious.

I relearned a lesson from my youth, namely "to tell the truth." Telling the truth sounds so easy, but, in fact, was extremely difficult and complex. For nearly two years I sat on the truth and kept it quiet out of fear and shame. I learned that the weight of a terrible, unspoken truth has incredible power—the power to crush and destroy me as well as those whom I love. It was only after the truth was out that I could begin the journey of healing by walking down the long, treacherous path of recovery and self-reclamation. I had to let go of the guilt caused by hiding the truth of Ally's abuse. Joe even used the fact that I'd not reported the abuse earlier as a weapon against me in a futile attempt to keep me quiet longer.

"Come on, Elly, you've known about the abuse for nearly two years; you're guilty, too! Don't spoil things now!" he spat at me. "My attorney is taking a look at the fact that you didn't report the abuse immediately when you found out about it," he continued.

I learned to "grow up." No longer could I live in a make-believe world shielded from reality. Not only did I have to squarely focus on the present, I had to also mop up the mistakes of the past—my past with Joe. In order to extricate myself from the muck and mire of sexual abuse I had to be aware of all the horrible things Joe did to Ally. I had to cry the tears, face the shame, and cradle my sobbing daughter. I had to admit that this did indeed happen to Ally, and that I was married to a pedophile who carefully manipulated us to maintain his sexual desires. I had to admit that I was naïve and yes, stupid. I had to deal with the bitterness, anger, and betrayal. It was horrible to "grow up" in this way, but I'm definitely a different, much more savvy and aware person now. No longer will I allow myself or my children or the children of others close to me to fall under the wily spell of a pedophile. I've learned to protect myself and be ever so vigilant with my children. Yes, we've all formed a shell of protection around us, but it is a healthy shell, penetrable only by those who genuinely love and respect us.

I've learned to breathe deeply when hopelessness takes over. I often felt like my whole body was literally bursting into teeny, shrunken-up pieces of an overly blown-up balloon that is suddenly popped. Only the intake of big gulps of air held me together. Sometimes I had to take in several elongated puffs of air in order to face the next piece of shrapnel being flung at me. For a while, I felt like all the well-meaning people in our lives just wanted a piece of my family and me. I felt like my friends just wanted to gobble up another juicy morsel so they could shake their heads and mutter, "how awful," and then go home and rejoice in how great *their* lives were! I didn't trust nor understand their solicitous looks. In addition, I just *knew* that the judges, lawyers, police, counselors, and medical people were all happy that this happened to my family and me so they could feel *important* in their jobs. I felt the sting of people's pitying glances and stares. I wanted to disappear in a land where no one knew about the abuse, and we could start again. I seriously considered moving and starting all over again in a new place, but I soon realized I had to face my problems *before* I could move ahead. Still, I wanted to throw my arms around my daughters and escape from everyone. Emotionally, I became so battered and beat up that I often simply forgot to breathe.

During the months of therapy my daughters and I came to realize that we could not rush the healing process. We had to take one agonizing step at a time, no matter how fast we wanted it to all disappear. The healing process began slowly with baby steps, which rapidly became leaps and bounds, as we began to regain our faith in God and our friends. We came out of this horrible experience stronger and changed people. The journey of healing was an amazing process. In the beginning Ally, June, and I were overwhelmed by the enormity and complexity of it all. How could we ever put ourselves back together again? Was it worth even trying? We were so tired and so hurt that the temptation to sit in a puddle of self-pity was very appealing. Even insanity sounded better than facing the healing process. I don't know for sure why we were able to begin the very scary road to recovery or how we were able to stay on it. Our religious faith was absolutely critical in the healing process, because there simply is no other explanation for our recovery.

My daughters and I are like everyone else, so we didn't possess any secrets or hidden strengths to help us through this, we just plodded along until the glimmer of joy gradually entered our lives. We started laughing and joking again and enjoying life. **Life's sweet joys returned as I crawled out of my miserable, bubbling cauldron of troubles.** I let myself hold Katy, one of our cats, as she softly purred and nuzzled me. I took a good hard look at my life and began to be thankful for all the wonderful things I *did* have. I lovingly looked at my beautiful daughters and current husband, and thought about how rich my life was because of them. Before I knew it, the good things in my life started overtaking the bad things, and I began to taste deep-down contentment like the sweet taste of rare, wild, juicy strawberries.

At first, I was afraid to taste this contentment because I thought it would be fleeting, and I was somehow setting myself up to be hurt again. Holding on to the pain had become a too-comfortable part of me. But the fleeting taste of contentment was sweeter than pain, and it won out. Eventually this sweet contentment became an integral part of me. I soon realized that all the painful baby steps I'd taken over the months and years of recovery were, in fact, a prerequisite for this lovely, sweet nectar of contentment. The journey of pain was the precious price I had to pay to experience contentment. In other words, I could never feel joy or happiness unless I could deal with the pain, resentment, and betrayal of sexual abuse. I continued to work diligently at putting the past in the past.

However, I also learned that the effects of sexual abuse are never really over. Unlike robbery, embezzlement, and grand theft, there is no real restitution for sexual crimes. Pedophiles can do prison time or participate in sexual offender programs, but they can't erase their victim's sad sexual memories or give them back lost innocence. Somewhere in the recesses of our brains, both Ally and I harbor unpleasant memories of early sexual abuse. That's just the way it is. We can't let it rule who we are. We have options as we choose to get on with our lives and lead good, happy lives. We can look to a better future, because we're smarter and know first-hand the devastation caused by sexual abuse.

Sadly, the aftermath of sexual abuse is forever. Ally, June, and I find it extremely difficult to trust anyone or form true, close bonds with others. Having been betrayed by the Abuser at a young age has, to a certain degree, messed up my notions of healthy sexual relationships. When I was a child I masturbated early and yearned for sexual stimulation, and when I became a teenager and boys noticed me, I was terrified of any closeness. In fact, when I was eighteen and was "making out" with my first bona fide boyfriend, I fainted and felt like throwing up. Then when I was a young woman in college, I wanted and sought approval by men, but did not trust any man until Joe. What a bad decision that was! I trusted Joe, even though I knew there was something dark and hidden deep within him. In fact, his dark side attracted me to him like a shiny lure attracts a naïve fish. I simply allowed myself to be reeled in! Joe's hidden secret resulted in a marriage devoid of a sexual relationship between him and me, sexual abuse of my daughter, Ally, and a long overdue divorce. It's only been for the past several years, during my second marriage to Thomas, that I've experienced a loving and intimate relationship.

It should be different for Ally, though. Hopefully, she will have better relationships with boys and men than I did. Ally got help through counseling, loving parents, and her faith. Unlike me, she didn't hold all of her abuse issues deep inside for decades. So I have every hope that Ally will lead a normal or close-to-normal adult life and will form healthy relationships with men. I also pray that she does not marry a closet pedophile like I did—I truly don't think she will.

Prayer for Chapter Thirteen

Dear Heavenly Father,

I pray for the courage to admit my sins and take full responsibility for the poor choices I've made. I thank you for saving me and for guiding me so I can learn from my mistakes and lead a better life. Thank you for making me humble enough to forgive. I especially thank you for helping my sweet Ally to forgive Joe. This means she can really get on with her life. Forgiving is so hard, so, Dear Father; help others to forgive abusers in their lives so they can dump the festering resentment that refusing to forgive brings.

Amen

CHAPTER 14
THE AFTERMATH

Turn from evil and do good: seek peace and pursue it.(Psalms 34:14)

If in field or tree,
There might only be
Such a warm, soft, sleepy place
Found for me!

    Unfortunately, the effects of sexual abuse are never really over. Even after ten years, Ally, June, and I still hurt. Although words cannot express the true depths of our pain, it remains forever a part of us. For me, the pain has changed over time and has taken several forms. For years after the sexual abuse by the Abuser, I stuffed the memories away like jamming clothes into a suitcase for trip that was never taken, foolishly thinking I could forget, but then when I discovered Joe's systematic and long-term sexual abuse of Ally, I had to deal not only with the stuffed-away past of the Abuser's abuse on me, but also the painful present of Joe's abuse on Ally. At first the pain was like a big ole hard knot wedged right in the middle of my chest—an ugly black monster with tentacles stretching throughout my entire body, through my arms to my fingertips and through my thighs, knees, and ankles to the tips of my toes. It was everywhere! I could taste the pain, which was similar to the disgusting aftertaste of severe acid reflux. Then, as time went on, the black tentacles shrunk and the hard black knot softened so that now, nearly ten years later, the pain is more like a deflated balloon that becomes inflated every time a memory returns. Sometimes the balloon is inflated by merely reading about an abused child in the newspaper or seeing a sweet little three-year-old girl playing in a park. You see, I was about three years old when the Abuser began sexually abusing me. Triggers are lurking everywhere from the sadness I see still mirrored in Ally's eyes in response to certain tastes, sounds, sights, and touches. When I see a man being very physical with a young daughter or niece, the memories flood back, and the balloon inflates. If I smell alcohol on someone's breath or they smell like cigarette smoke I think of the Abuser and how he groaned as he groped me. When I taste a sweet root beer barrel, a fireball, or a butterscotch candy, I think of how the Abuser brought us kids candy. Then sadness creeps in as I wonder why the Abuser chose to trade in my total trust and sweet love for incest and mere sexual satisfaction. Sometimes when I meet a man for the first time and I shake hands, I get cold vibes that permeate my hand then my arm like lightening coursing through my veins to my heart. I've finally learned to trust my feelings! I've learned to stay away from men such as these and to keep my daughters away from them. The effects of sexual abuse will remain with Ally and me throughout our lives, but we've now learned to protect ourselves from pedophiles and to walk away from situations that "just don't feel right."

Even though it's been nearly ten years since Joe made the report to the Child Protective Services, our saga continues as real effects of sexual abuse weave their way through the tightly woven fabric of our lives. We've all felt the long-reaching, nasty effects of Joe's actions.

Just a few years ago, Ally was back in counseling for stress-related problems. She pulled out all her eyelashes and yanked out her hair strand by strand, leaving a half-dollar bald spot on the back of her head. The counselor said this was due to stress, perhaps post-traumatic stress from Joe's sexual abuse. She also frequently "spaces out" as if she's in a trance, living in a far away world. Even as a teenager, Ally is slow to really trust others and feels defeated when challenged. This I understand. She'd rather not be challenged than to put forth the effort and fail. Academically, Ally has done well, even though she gets frustrated if she doesn't grasp an idea quickly. She often has difficulty following through to completion of a task and is easily distracted by other things. She escapes by retreating to a make-believe world through reading, play, and music.

Although she was forbidden to date until she was at least fifteen, at fourteen she became interested in boys and had friends who were boys. She has several close friends and is well liked at school. When given the opportunity she still likes to dress sexy, revealing her midriff or wearing tight clothing. She rarely talks about Joe or what he did to her other than wondering what will happen to Joe after he completes the program.

Recently Ally asked, "Mom, what will happen to Joe after he finishes the sexual offender program he is in? Can he live anywhere he wants to after his treatment is over? Can he come after me? Can he be around children again?"

I reassured her that there is a restraining order against Joe for Ally's entire life so he can't have any contact with her.

Ally often tosses and turns in her sleep, in fact, so much so that she frequently smashes into the wall by her bed. She still has the terrifying nightmares about a scary entity going after her, but now she's not so scared because she has some secret and magical force that wards off evil. Unlike the nightmares she had before her counseling and the CPS report, she knows that she will not be caught in these later nightmares. I can only surmise that she is dealing with the stuff of her life as she sleeps.

My other daughter June has also felt the effects left in Joe's wake. Interesting enough Lucy, Joe's sexual offenders program counselor, recently told me that often it is the daughter who was not sexually abused that has horrible teenage years. June has been to several counselors for anorexia, anger management, body dysmorphic disorder and severe depression. She has been on medication for obsessive-compulsive disorder, attention deficit disorder, depression, psychosis, and anxiety. June has ongoing problems relating to her peers and family. She rarely exhibits genuine affection and doesn't laugh often. Despite natural prettiness she insists she is grotesquely ugly and chooses to hide behind a mask of make-up and insecurity. She's so afraid to let the world see who she really is. Although we've taken her to four therapists and three psychiatrists, she refuses to work with them and insists she is fine as she stubbornly refuses help. She is an ice princess in the family and doesn't show affection or emotion toward, Thomas, Ally, or me. She, too, does well academically but is either driven to perfection or totally gives up. She often puts forth ten times the effort required on her schoolwork. June has unrealistic expectations for a boyfriend and rigidly holds on to her ideal of the perfect "hotty." Certainly some of June's behavior is due to normal teenage development and who she is, but the extremes of her behavior are related to the relinquishment by her birth parents and Joe, the huge life changes brought about because of Joe's sexual abuse of Ally, and the fact that beloved relatives of Joe severed their relationship with her. June became so physically abusive to the family that upon Thomas's and my request she was arrested and spent one night in a juvenile corrections facility.

June, too, has strange dreams. In her dreams, she flies around and around in rooms with tall ceilings without ever reaching her destination. She has other dreams in which, she, like Ally, possesses magic tools, like a magic hole punch that protects her and holds the secret of safety.

Like my daughters, I am not left unscathed by the talons of sexual abuse. I am taking anti-anxiety medication to help reduce anxieties I've felt since childhood. My doctor said I am probably suffering from post-traumatic stress caused by the emotional upheaval of dealing with the sexual abuse issues of the Abuser and my ex-husband. Now I wish I'd taken medication earlier when my counselors and doctors recommended it, but I stubbornly refused for five years! I have dreams of great sadness during which I am sucked into a dark hole in the ground. Struggling, I always claw my way out of the hole but feel the great weight of pain and sadness as the force in the hole continues to try to swallow me up and suck me in.

Thomas, too, has felt the effects of Joe's abuse. Thomas is angry with Joe for the sadness and pain he selfishly inflicted on Ally, June, and me. Thomas's testosterone level rises as he expresses the inner desire to punch Joe with a blow that would rock the earth! Thomas, of course, realizes that this would be a temporary relief, and there is nothing he can do to erase the pain Joe caused. Assault charges would only open up wounds better left alone. Right now it's enough for Thomas to know that Joe is being held accountable for his actions. We stay away from the community where Joe lives and do not contact him. Thomas offers Ally, June, and me the love we never had with Joe.

In spite of it all, my family and I face each day with incredible love and understanding for each other. This love helps us to be the strong parents we must be to cope with the pitfalls our daughters experience as they travel the bumpy road of growing up. We've gained Herculean strength and deep-down courage to handle life and its painful twists, because together we survived. We've been given the wonderful opportunity to live life to its fullest and to taste the sweet happiness now in our possession. Fully armed with God's love, faith, lessons learned, haunting memories, and jagged scars etched in my heart and soul, I embrace life and am driven to help other victims emerge from the deep, dark abyss of sexual abuse.

Prayer for Chapter Fourteen

Dear Father God,

Today I pray for my family's future. Help us to deal with the hurt of the past so we can joyfully embrace the future. I also pray for all the childhood victims of sexual abuse so they can now reap Your blessings. Help us to seek out those you have put in our lives to help us, and help us to listen to You so we don't fall victim to other forms of abuse. Help us to forgive those who have hurt us and to trust those whose true spirits are to help us. Finally, help us to turn to you in times of pain so Your healing can comfort us.

Amen

EPILOGUE

Now my daughters are attending college. Ally has recovered well, primarily because she embraced Christianity wholeheartedly. Ally is studying to become a science teacher of junior high school students, but her ultimate goal is to become a youth pastor. So far she's had healthy relationships with young men in college and dates only Christian men. Ally is happy and jubilantly greets each new day. She loves the college Christian group and is actively involved in charitable activities. The effects of the abuse are not visible in her day-to-day life, but she told me the effects are still there, nonetheless. She is passionate about stemming the spread of sexual abuse.

June is twenty years old and is also attending college. She wants to teach English to Spanish-speaking people. She craves male attention and struggles with male relationships and dating. She wants young men to really love her, but she doesn't know whether the men she dates are sincere or not. June wants to make people happy, and will sacrifice her own needs and desires for others. I think she desires male attention, in part, because as a young girl she was locked out of the bedroom and left alone while Joe sexually abused Ally.

Joe has finished his eight-and-a-half-year sentence in the community-based sexual-offender program but continues to attend meetings and classes voluntarily. He must register as a sex offender with law enforcement agencies wherever he resides. He recently told me that the best thing that ever happened to him was getting caught. Although still not a Christian, much of his former arrogance is replaced with remorse and even humility.

As for me, I recently recovered from breast cancer, and I continue to teach. The lives of my own children and my schoolchildren keep me active and blessed. Despite some bumps along the way, my marriage to Thomas is wonderful. We continue to grow closer to each other as we worship and pray together daily. God continues to shower us with love and joy as we recognize the amazing miracles he places in our daily lives. We believe we have nothing to fear because, like the following Bible verse says, we know God will never leave us.

God has said, "Never will I leave you: never will I forsake you." So we say with confidence, "The Lord is my helper; I will not be afraid, What can man do to me?" (Hebrews 13:5-6)